D0866597

The Analysis of the Transference in the Here and Now

The Analysis of the Transference in the Here and Now

GREGORY P. BAUER, Ph.D.

JASON ARONSON INC.
Northvale, New Jersey
London

The author gratefully acknowledges permission to reprint material from the following sources:

Excerpts from "The Therapeutic Use of Countertransference Data with Borderline Patients," by L. Epstein, in *Contemporary Psychoanalysis*, vol. 15, pp. 248–275. Copyright © 1979 by *Contemporary Psychoanalysis*. Reprinted by permission.

Excerpts from "The Dynamics of Transference," "On Beginning the Treatment," and "Remembering, Repeating, and Working Through" by Sigmund Freud. (*Standard Edition*, volume 12). Copyright © by Sigmund Freud Copyrights, The Institute of Psycho-Analysis, and The Hogarth Press. Permission to quote from *The Standard Edition of the Complete Psychological Works of Sigmund Freud*, translated and edited by James Strachey, has been granted by Random House UK Limited and Basic Books.

Excerpts from "The Nature of the Therapeutic Action of Psychoanalysis," by James Strachey, in *International Journal of Psycho-Analysis*, vol. 15, pp. 127–159. Copyright © 1934 by the Institute of Psycho-Analysis. Reprinted by permission.

Quotation from from Harry Stack Sullivan in unpublished material held by the Washington School of Psychiatry and quoted in *The Contributions of Harry Stack Sullivan*, edited by Patrick Mullahy. Used by permission of the Washington School of Psychiatry.

This book is set in 12 point Goudy by Lind Graphics of Upper Saddle River, New Jersey, and printed and bound by Haddon Craftsmen of Scranton, Pennsylvania.

Copyright © 1993 by Jason Aronson Inc.

10 9 8 7 6 5 4 3 2 1

All rights reserved. Printed in the United States of America. No part of this book may be used or reproduced in any manner whatsoever without written permission from Jason Aronson Inc. except in the case of brief quotations in reviews for inclusion in a magazine, newspaper, or broadcast.

Library of Congress Cataloging-in-Publication Data

Bauer, Gregory P.
   The analysis of the transference in the here and now / by Gregory
P. Bauer.
      p. cm.
   Includes bibliographical references and index.
   ISBN 0-87668-143-7
   1. Transference (Psychology) I. Title.
   [DNLM: 1. Psychoanalytic Interpretation. 2. Transference
(Psychology) WM 62 B344a]
   RC489.T73B38 1993
   616–dc20
   DNLM/DLC
   for Library of Congress   92-49521

Manufactured in the United States of America. Jason Aronson Inc. offers books and cassettes. For information and catalog write to Jason Aronson Inc., 230 Livingston Street, Northvale, New Jersey 07647.

For Kathy,
Carl, Aaron, and Samuel

Contents

Chapter Two

The Importance of the Analysis of Transference in the
Here and Now   11

The Here and Now Is Emotionally Immediate/The
Here and Now Reflects Both Current and Past
Relations/Transference Versus Extratransference
Interpretation/Freud's Use of Transference

Part II
PATIENT-CENTERED RESISTANCE   25

Chapter Three

Overview of Resistance   27

Definition and Description/Why the Patient
Resists/Therapist Stance toward Resistance

Chapter Four

Patient Resistance to the Analysis of Transference in the
Here and Now   39

Resistance to Transference Awareness/Why the Patient
Avoids Awareness of Transference/Helping the Patient
Become More Aware of Transference: Patient Preparation/
Therapist Stance/Identifying Transference: Allusions to
Transference/Patient Resistance to Transference Awareness:
Fear of Ignoring Real Life Concerns/Resistance to
Transference Resolution/Resistance to Remembering (and
Facing Oneself)/Resistance to Collaboration and Mature
Interchange (and Facing the Present Moment)/Resistance to
Autonomy (and Facing Responsibility)

Part III
THERAPIST-CENTERED RESISTANCE   61

Part IV
TECHNIQUE OF DEALING WITH TRANSFERENCE   155

Acknowledgments

I would like to acknowledge my gratitude to those authors appearing in the References. I found their writings to be stimulating and of consequence. I wish to thank Gerald Thorner, a supervisor, friend, and colleague who critically influenced my conceptualization of the therapeutic interaction and the use of the here and now. I wish to thank Virginia Crandell, whose patience, dedication, and outstanding typing skills were of immeasurable value. An additional thanks is extended to Jason Aronson for his enthusiasm, encouragement, and helpful suggestions.

To my wife, Kathy, and my sons, Carl, Aaron, and Samuel, I wish to express a special thanks for their love, patience, and unwavering support.

Preface

Sandor Ferenczi once observed that most innovations in technique are not new and are already part of the practitioner's repertoire.[1] The current work does not seek to demonstrate new revelations regarding use of transference but rather to sensitize and shed greater light on the difficulties involved in its here-and-now analysis. While given seminal consideration in theory, such analysis is often underemphasized in clinical practice.

Here-and-now work with transference material is an emotionally potent experience for both patient and therapist. Anxieties and misunderstandings in both patient and therapist may lead them to resist this focus. Transference can be a powerful therapeutic tool; it is important to be aware of impediments to effective intervention.

Gregory P. Bauer
Stevens Point, Wisconsin, 1993

Part I

Importance and Overview

Chapter One

Overview

Transference, which seems ordained to be the greatest obstacle to psycho-analysis, becomes its most powerful ally, if its presence can be detected each time and explained to the patient.

Sigmund Freud, 1905, p. 117

Transference, as applied to the psychotherapeutic process, refers to the manner in which the patient's conscious and preconscious reactions to the therapist are influenced by the patient's internalized representations of self and others, particularly one's early childhood objects. The analysis of transference reactions is generally acknowledged as the central feature of psychoanalytically informed technique. The understanding and interpretation of transference reactions was stressed by Freud as the vehicle of cure in psychoanalytic treatment.[1] As Freud described it, transference played the central role of bringing to awareness repressed, hidden conflict, and of furnishing an arena in which resolution can be attempted.

Analysis of transference involves an interpretive focus on three relationship situations: (1) past relationships of childhood, (2) current relationships with present-day objects, and (3) the immediate here-and-now relationship between patient and therapist. The traditional transference interpretation reconstructs the past and explains how it affects the present patient–therapist interaction.

EARLY TRENDS: THE TRANSFERENCE NEUROSIS

Early psychodynamic trends in transference intervention emphasized understanding and reconstructing the genetic development of psychic conflict; psychotherapy was a process of uncovering the past psychic origin of present-day conflict. Technical interventions were geared to ensure the maximal development of the transference neurosis, which was seen as the most important vehicle of success in classical analytic technique.[2] The transference neurosis was viewed as a reenactment of the essential conflicts of the infantile neurosis in a current setting. Once established and identified, the classical analyst worked to reduce the transference neurosis to its genetic origin. This was accomplished first through an examination of transference and relative resistances, and eventually by means of genetic interpretations, recollections and reconstructions, and working through. "As the transference is related to its genetic origins, the analyst thereby emerges in his true, i.e., real, identity to the patient; the transference is putatively 'resolved.' "[3]

An artifact of the analytic situation as engineered by Freud, the transference neurosis was facilitated by the use of the couch, daily sessions, therapist anonymity, nonintrusiveness and passivity, and the rules of abstinence and free association.[4] In this approach the therapist was viewed as a neutral, opaque, relatively unobtrusive figure upon which the patient's unresolved libidinal and aggressive conflicts were projected, thus allowing for their reconstruction and working through.[1] Although often effective in deepening the patient's self-understanding and sense of identity, the development of a regressive transference relationship emphasizing genetic recovery has been criticized as significantly lengthening treatment and resulting in less than optimal behavioral change.[5,6,7]

CURRENT TRENDS: THE HERE AND NOW

In early psychodynamic work, with its focus on the recovery of genetic material, the therapist–patient relationship was used as a way of gaining access to repressed material of the past. Of late there has been increased interest in a more active use of the transference relationship as a vehicle for modification of maladaptive coping strategies displaced onto the therapy situation.[8,9] This approach to the use of transference has been termed the *analysis of the transference in the here and now*[10] and highlights the use of the current here-and-now relationship between patient and therapist to clarify, examine, and modify interpersonal conflict rather than as a springboard for discussing the genetic determinants of conflict. This approach strives to change the psychotherapeutic setting from one where the therapist acts upon the patient by an analysis of his intrapsychic processes, to a mutual and collaborative examination of the nature of their relationship and interaction patterns.

An important impetus for development in the here-and-now use of transference comes from the burgeoning field of short-term psychotherapy. There has been a steady increase of interest and demand for effective modes of short-term treatment. Strupp and Binder contend that a focus on the here-and-now interaction is a critical component of techniques in brief, dynamic psychotherapy.[8] Bauer and Kobos, in a review of major contributors to the development of short-term dynamic psychotherapy (e.g., Davanloo, Malan, Sifneos), posit that the crucial change agent common to their techniques was an intensive focus on interpretation and working through of the transference relationship.[11] This emphasis is reflected in Davanloo's description of modern dynamic treatment as an attempt to identify, understand, and resolve the reciprocal interactive process occurring between patient and therapist, rather than an analysis of the psychic contents of the mind as presented through free association.[12] The immediate patient–therapist relationship is used to learn about the patient's various patterns of relating with others. Although identifying similar patterns of behavior in past and current functioning is important in transference resolution, the critical focus is on the use of the patient–therapist relationship for modification of conflictual patterns of relating. The immediate interpersonal relationship between patient and therapist is utilized to correct persistent maladaptive coping strategies created by an interpersonal relationship of the past.[13]

DEFINITION OF HERE-AND-NOW WORK

Work with transference in the here and now includes (1) sensitizing patients to the importance of examining their reactions to the therapist; (2) identifying the constricted, self-defeating components of these patterns; and (3) developing an increasingly flexible and mature interaction with the therapist. The focus is on transference reactions, or patterns of behavior that are transference based, rather than a systematic development and interpretation of a highly organized set of fantasies and attitudes displaced onto the therapist (i.e., the transference neurosis). Although existing on a continuum with the regressive transference neurosis, transference reactions are less organized, less intense, and less pervasive.

The here-and-now approach deemphasizes gaining access to repressed infantile conflict through intentional facilitation of a transference neurosis. Instead, major emphasis is placed on the examination and working through of characteristic patterns of relating to others that are self-defeating and maladaptive. Rather than being abstinent to promote a transference neurosis, the therapist actively examines the patient–therapist interaction to assist the patient in understanding the development, maintenance, and implications of his interactional style.

Early interaction patterns that protected security and reduced anxiety tend to be used and reused in new relationships, often to the detriment of the individual. In the analysis of transference in the here and now, great importance is placed on helping the patient observe and reconsider characteristic patterns of interacting. Therapist and patient work to clarify what is occurring between them and how effective their interaction is in meeting mature and realistic needs. When such interaction is problematic, efforts are made to develop a relationship that is less conflictual. This work is facilitated by helping the patient look at how the transfer or displacement of previously learned attitudes, expectations, and coping strategies may distort the present relationship and constrict his interaction possibilities. Examination of the patient's interpersonal relatedness does not preclude intrapsychic work (i.e., the focus on internal conflict and the mental processes that give rise to it). In pointing out what has transpired between them, the therapist can help the patient to recognize a pattern to his personal relations and to see how this pattern relates to the more private states that are also a central concern of therapy.[14]

RESISTANCE TO HERE-AND-NOW ANALYSIS

The notion of vigorous here-and-now use of transference reactions is not new. As early as 1925, Rank and Ferenczi, in their classic volume on analytic technique, emphasized using the immediate, here-and-now relationship to clarify, examine, and modify interpersonal conflict, rather than as a springboard for discussing the developmental history of a patient.[15] The focus on patient defenses, transference reactions, and the deemphasis of genetic insight, was felt by Rank and Ferenczi to heighten the emotional immediacy and relevance of feelings and behaviors. The work of other early analysts such as Reich on "resistance analysis," and Alexander on the "corrective emotional experience" similarly echoes the importance of attention to the patient–therapist interaction as a means of promoting change.[16,5] Interpersonal and object relation theorists (e.g., Sullivan, Racker, and Kernberg) have also consistently stressed the importance of careful attention to the development and enactment of conflictual interpersonal strategies within the treatment relationship.[17,18,19] The writings of other analysts such as Wachtel, Schafer and, perhaps most importantly, Gill, offer further support for this approach.[20,21,22]

Despite the theoretical attention given to the concept of transference and to its use in the therapeutic process, Gill contends that it is often underemphasized in clinical practice.[22] Analysis of transference, he argues, is not pursued as systematically and comprehensively as would be optimal; while most psychodynamic therapists would agree that transference is of central importance, its application is tentative.

Although it has been observed that "nothing about analysis is less well known than how individual analysts actually use transference in their day-to-day work with patients"[23] it has been my experience through teaching, supervising, and consulting with colleagues that active, here-and-now use of transference material is indeed underemphasized, often to the detriment of the patient's opportunity for change and growth. It is my contention that differences between theory and practice stem from resistances within the patient *and* the therapist. The remainder of this book will seek to highlight both the motivations and the means by which patient and therapist may resist a focus on their transference relationship. As these resistances are elucidated, principles of here-and-now work will be developed and applied.

Chapter Two

The Importance of the Analysis of Transference in the Here and Now

It cannot be disputed that controlling the phenomena of transference presents the psycho-analyst with the greatest difficulties. But it should not be forgotten that it is precisely they that do us the inestimable service of making the patient's hidden and forgotten erotic impulses immediate and manifest. For when all is said and done, it is impossible to destroy anyone in absentia or in effigie.

Sigmund Freud, 1912a, p. 108

Analysis of transference reactions in the here and now may contribute to an effective therapeutic outcome in the following ways: (1) here-and-now work is an emotionally immediate, experience–near endeavor which engages the patient's feelings in a productive manner; (2) the here-and-now transference relationship provides a vehicle by which the patient's typical means of reacting and interacting may be examined and modified; and (3) the interpretations of here-and-now transference reactions are potentially more accurate, potent, and more open to mutual discussion and validation than are interpretations regarding the patient's past or current life unrelated to his transference experience.

THE HERE AND NOW IS EMOTIONALLY IMMEDIATE

> *Every mutative [change-inducing] interpretation must be emotionally "immediate"; the patient must experience it as something actual.*
>
> James Strachey, 1934, p. 150

Empirical research and clinical experience teach that optimal learning occurs when one's attention and feelings are engaged. Luborsky and colleagues found that of all the measures of psychotherapy process, level of patient experience was the most successful in predicting outcome.[1] Orlinsky and Howard concluded that a high level of patient experience was consistently predictive of therapeutic success.[2] Similarly, Davenloo found a positive correlation between a high level of emotional involvement and successful outcome.[3] To be most effective the psychotherapy framework must foster an emotionally meaningful experience.

Psychodynamic approaches to therapy have been criticized throughout their history for an overreliance on insight to induce change and promote growth. A focus on insight, according to critics, runs the risk of an abstract, intellectualized, and experience-distant approach to the patient. Such a stance often leads to a less than optimal level of emotional engagement and a less impactful therapy. Work with transference in the here and now offers the opportunity for a more optimal level of emotional engagement. This work is affectively immediate. The examination of immediate-in-therapy behavior is more emotionally compelling than a description of behavior or events outside therapy.[4] In a discussion of what is change-inducing in psychodynamic treatment, Strupp argues that there is nothing as vivid and as meaningful to a patient as present-day events, especially events transpiring in the powerfully charged patient-therapist relationship which revive the basic primitive components of the child–parent relationship.[5] He further observes that critics of psychoanalysis, as well as many of its practitioners, have frequently misunderstood the fulcrum upon which the therapeutic action turns. Psychotherapeutic change, according to Strupp, does not depend on the uncovering of historical antecedents but on the modification of historically meaningful patterns that come alive in the patient–therapist relationship. Here-and-now work doesn't deny the importance of the past or current outside life but attempts to maximize the efficiency and power of the therapeutic interchange. It is seen as the power cell of the treatment.[6]

A higher level of emotional experience does not always result in a more satisfactory therapeutic outcome. More is not always better. Too much or too little affect interferes with the process of therapy. If the patient is too relaxed, if a conflict is not active, or if a patient is too well defended, nothing happens; on the other hand, if too much anxiety exists, if a patient is too flooded with affect, or his reality situation is too chaotic, the treatment will bog down. Indeed, much of therapy revolves around the therapist's attempt to find and maintain an optimal level of therapeutic tension and affective engagement. Optimal therapeutic tension varies from patient to patient. People differ in the degree to which they can sustain productive functioning in the face of anxiety and emotional impact.

THE HERE AND NOW REFLECTS BOTH CURRENT AND PAST RELATIONS

Each of an individual's relationships reflects the others; it is rare . . . for one to be able to relate in bad faith to some individuals and in an authentic, caring way to a select few.
Irvin Yalom, 1980, p. 390

A primary assumption in here-and-now work is that given the establishment of a conducive therapeutic environment, the patient's problematic and conflicted coping strategies will be reenacted in the therapeutic relationship, allowing for examination, understanding, and modification. The patient (and often, the novice therapist), may be hesitant to believe that one's interpersonal problems will be repeated in the therapy. After all, the therapist is a much different person than those other individuals in the person's life, so much more understanding, sensitive, and perceptive. But given time, provided the therapist is optimally neutral, neither overindulgent nor unduly frustrating, and provided a here-and-now transference focus is encouraged and maintained, the therapeutic relationship will begin, sometimes quickly, other times gradually, to resemble aspects of other relationships in the patient's life. Conflicts experienced with past and present relationships will come alive within the therapeutic dyad. With time a here-and-now focus allows the patient to see that difficulties experienced with the therapist, in being a patient, in working collaboratively, are no different than the difficulties encountered in other relationships. When the patient confronts his resistive strategies within therapy he will usually find analogous problems and impasses in past and present relationships.[7]

The patient gradually comes to realize that the therapeutic relationship will portray the problems in relatedness that the patient comes to therapy to work on. The patient–therapist interaction often becomes the best place to examine the patient's maladaptive means of organizing experience and relating to others. To the extent difficulties in relating between patient and therapist are overcome, the patient is in a better position to do this in other relationships.[8]

Menninger writes of the importance for the patient to actually *experience* with the therapist his conflicted attempts to meet his needs. He points out that in good time the patient's self-defeating interpersonal relations will be pointed out, if he doesn't recognize them himself. "But first he must experience them, see and feel the ways in which he tries to get what he wants. He will ultimately realize that certain methods, constantly unsuccessful, nevertheless were retained by him, whereas better ones were abandoned because under certain circumstances—one particularly painful time, maybe—they didn't work."[9] Here-and-now work offers the patient the experiential opportunity to discover for himself that certain behavior is anachronistic, often self-defeating, and no longer appropriate. This, according to Wolf, is the essence of the analysis of the transference.[10]

A goal of here-and-now work is to encourage the expression of the patient's conflicted means of attempting to meet his needs in the relationship with the therapist. The therapist encourages the transference to expand within the session by focusing on the patient's resistance to identifying and acknowledging transference. This is a critical component of treatment. As Freud points out, once transference is expressed in the treatment it is accessible to our intervention.[11] In similar fashion, Strachey states that when conflicts are reenacted in relation to the therapist, we have a great opportunity to explore and modify them,

> instead of having to deal as best we may with conflicts of the remote past, which are concerned with dead circumstances and mummified personalities, and whose outcome is already determined, we find ourselves involved in an actual and immediate situation, in which we and the patient are the principal characters and the development of which is to some extent at least under our control.[12]

What does the here-and-now learning process consist of? Yalom suggests a rotating sequence of evoking affect by means of the interaction, followed by an examination of that affect.[6] The here-and-now focus provides the patient an opportunity to experience his interpersonal difficulties and also to examine *in vivo* the how and why of these difficulties with a skilled participant–observer. If just the experience is the focus, the therapy may seem exciting but little learning will be entailed. If the focus is strictly on examination and understanding, therapy will become sterile, rigid, and intellectual. In effective treatment, the patient must experience an affect *and* see himself in action.

> Just as a tennis coach cannot correct a student's errors until both can observe them in the course of a game, patient and therapist must become engaged in an interaction before mutative change can occur. First, the patient must act; then with the help of the therapist, he or she must step back and observe the action; finally, the meaning and purpose of the action must be explored.[13]

A here-and-now focus facilitates learning in additional ways: (1) interchange reduces the likelihood of inaccurate communication and misinterpretation; (2) the opportunity is presented where anxieties and uncertainties in the relationship may be brought to a conscious, verbal level versus being acted out; (3) explicit discussion of the relationship decreases the tendency for a nonverbal manipulation to obtain what is wanted; (4) discussion of one's immediate thoughts and feelings helps the patient sort out his identity by having to express it; the patient is offered the ego-enhancing opportunity to clarify for self and others who he is; (5) a powerful model is provided for the patient to use in other relationships.[14]

TRANSFERENCE VERSUS EXTRATRANSFERENCE INTERPRETATION

> *If I may take an analogy from trench warfare, the acceptance of a transference interpretation corresponds to the capture of a key position, while the extra-transference interpretations correspond to the general advance and to the consolidation of a fresh line which are made possible by the capture of the key position. But when this general advance goes beyond a certain point, there will be another check, and*

the capture of a further key position will be necessary before progress can be resumed. An oscillation of this kind between transference and extratransference interpretations will represent the normal course of events in an analysis.

James Strachey, 1934, p. 158

In analysis of transference in the here and now the transference interpretation takes precedence over the extratransference interpretation (i.e., an interpretation regarding the patient's past or current life unrelated to his transference experience). A transference interpretation is liable to be both more effective and less risky than an extratransference interpretation.[12] It is likely to be more effective because it is affectively immediate; it concerns an impulse being felt and expressed toward one who is currently present. Conversely, an extratransference interpretation tends to be concerned with impulses that are distant both in time and space and are thus likely to be devoid of immediate energy. A transference interpretation is less risky and likely to be more accurate because the events examined in a here-and-now transference interpretation are better known than the events of an extratransference (genetic or contemporary) interpretation.

A here-and-now focus provides a more reliable source of information regarding the patient than does a recount of one's past or contemporary life. Work on the latter is often difficult because you have incomplete or biased (intentionally or unintentionally) data. Discussion of outside events is susceptible to the patient's particular defensive organization, which impacts his perceptual and communications abilities. With a transference interpretation both patient and therapist have firsthand knowledge of the actual experience and thus are in a more optimal place for a mutual examination, as opposed to a situation where one has to rely on the input of the other before any impressions can be formed. "No other interpretation is free, within reason, of the doubt introduced by not really knowing the 'other person's' participation in love, or quarrel, or criticism, or whatever the issue."[15]

Because the transference experience is more emotionally immediate and because the patient's reaction is about someone actually present, the patient has a greater opportunity to become aware of potential differences between his internal representations of objects and the actual, reality object, that is, the therapist. It is easier for the patient to examine the difference between what he expects in his relationship with the therapist and what actually occurs, than it is to examine these same points with a past or contemporary object that is not actually present. Analysis of the here-and-now situation allows the patient to check out to see if his reactions are a realistic response to another and if need be, undergo necessary learning and modification. Such work is more difficult when attempting to examine the "there and then."

Writing in support of a transference versus an extratransference interpretation, Greenacre identifies a further complication in an interpretative focus on the patient's outside relations.[16] An attempt by the therapist to objectively define the patient's outside relations may result in the therapist examining the patient's whole situation and the various people in it rather than focusing on analysis of the patient and his attitudes toward various aspects of his life. This decreases the potential of the therapy to help the patient understand himself. The patient may imitate the therapist's stance and, instead of focusing on himself and questioning his own attitudes, begin to deflect his concern and interpret the unconscious motivations of those around him. Unless it is recognized, the therapist may unwittingly furnish the patient with a set of tools intended for self-understanding but misappropriated and used for resistance against such under-standing. Greenacre considers this one of the easiest and most destructive bypaths away from a thorough analysis.

It is not that extratransference interpretations have no value and should be set aside. Their importance in the therapy must not be underestimated; they are often highly successful in facilitating increased insight and in providing a therapeutic hold by means of accurate empathy. Attention to outside relations is important in that not all relationship tendencies will find ex-pression within the patient–therapist relationship. The therapist can learn much regarding the patient's adaptive and defensive functioning through the discussion of outside relationships. Also, there are many times when a particular behavioral inter-action is easier to discuss in relationship to a third person. A discussion of the here and now may, with some patients, and at some points in therapy, create greater than optimal therapeutic tension and become unproductive. H. S. Sullivan was particu-larly sensitive to this and often spent much time analyzing the patient's outside relations before focusing on the patient–thera-pist dyad.[17] It must be noted, however, that Sullivan did much of his work with a rather disturbed population of patients, in particular those with schizophrenic and severe obsessive-com-pulsive personality disorders.

A focus on outside relations allows the therapist to learn more about the potential transferences that may develop within therapy, enabling the therapist to become more alert for their within-session manifestations. The patient, for instance, who complains of being misunderstood by significant others pos-sesses strong potential to replicate this experience with the therapist. Prior discussion of this feeling in outside relations may sensitize the therapist to its occurrence in the here and now. The therapist and patient may use what is learned regarding the patient's other relationships to more accurately understand their own. An extratransference interpretation often may be used as a prelude to a transference interpretation.

The danger of an extended focus on outside relations and of extratransference interpretations is that they foster intellectualization because they are not affectively immediate. And, as is often the case, an extratransference interpretation may be offered in a situation where a more direct here-and-now discussion is warranted—a flight from the immediacy of the moment is made. The implied message is that there is some danger in an honest and genuine encounter between patient and therapist.

> *Giving non-transference-interpretations is, in fact, like trying to untie a knot in an endless ring or rope. You can untie the knot quite easily in one place, but it will re-tie itself at the very same moment in some other part of the ring. You cannot really untie the knot unless you have hold of the ends of the rope, and that is your situation only when you make a transference-interpretation.*
>
> James Strachey, 1937, p. 143

FREUD'S USE OF TRANSFERENCE

Although Freud firmly anchored analytic technique to the transference experience, a perusal of his writings may leave one unclear as to exactly how Freud used transference in his treatment. Gill posits that Freud's case reports were designed to demonstrate the yield of the analysis for the structure and function of the psyche, not the technique by which this yield was acquired. "More interested in presenting the dynamic of the neurosis . . . Freud felt that it would be impossible to give the mass of detail necessary to show the analytic work."[18] Wachtel argues that Freud emphasized the patient's intrapsychic processes, the inner life, more so than interpersonal transactions.[19] Even with Freud's strong focus on transference, which would seem to imply great attention to the interpersonal, Wachtel suggests that Freud did not look much at interaction sequences or consider how present behavior and its consequences perpetuate old patterns. When a patient's interpersonal relation became a focus of investigation, it tended to be of interest for what could be learned from it regarding its underlying dynamics.

Although the importance of transference work was underscored in Freud's papers on technique, one cannot be sure if the analysis of transference was often ancillary to work outside the transference and primarily important as an avenue to the patient's inner psychology—or, on the other hand, if it was assigned a central role in which the patient experiences, identifies, and works through his/her neurotic struggle. "It is on that field that the victory must be won. The victory whose expression is the permanent cure of the neurosis."[20]

Part II

Patient-Centered Resistance

Chapter Three

Overview of Resistance

It is a long superseded idea, and one derived from superficial appearances, that the patient suffers from a sort of ignorance, and that if one removes this ignorance by giving him information (about the causal connection of his illness with his life, about his experiences in childhood, and so on) he is bound to recover. The pathological factor is not his ignorance in itself, but the root of this ignorance in his inner resistances; it was they that first called this ignorance into being and they still maintain it now. The task of the treatment lies in combating these resistances. Informing the patient of what he does not know because he repressed it is only one of the necessary preliminaries to the treatment. If knowledge about the unconscious were as important for the patient as people inexperienced in psychoanalysis imagine, listening to lectures or reading books would be enough to cure him. Such measures, however, have as much influence on the symptoms of nervous illness as a distribution of menu-cards in a time of famine has upon hunger.

Sigmund Freud, 1910, p. 225

While there has been considerable evolution in theoretical notions regarding the most efficacious use of psychodynamically oriented psychotherapy, practical implementation often lags behind. This is seen to be the case for analysis of transference reactions. Differences between theory and practice are viewed as stemming from resistances within patient and therapist to the identification and examination of the here-and-now therapeutic relationship. Although resistance is typically conceptualized and discussed as being primarily a patient phenomenon, that is, a reaction of the patient to therapy, it is felt that the therapist may also resist the therapeutic process, particularly here-and-now work with transference material. Often neither party wants to face the possible implications of their reactions, afraid of damaging the relationship by discussing anxiety-provoking feelings or perhaps changing the relationship when gratifying interactions are involved. In this chapter the concept of resistance will be discussed. In subsequent chapters, key resistances to transference analysis will be highlighted.

DEFINITION AND DESCRIPTION

This working-through of the resistances may in practice turn out to be an arduous task . . . and a trial of patience for the analyst. Nevertheless it is a part of the work which effects the greatest changes in the patient and which distinguishes analytic treatment from any kind of treatment by suggestion.

Sigmund Freud, 1914, pp. 155-156

The concept of resistance is age-old and of integral concern in psychodynamic psychotherapy. It may be defined as any behavior in therapy that interferes with the process of uncovering, affective expression, and working through of patient conflicts. Resistive behavior is an impediment to an effective therapist–patient collaboration on resolving patient problems.

Resistance is omnipresent in the psychotherapy process. Freud observed that resistance to treatment accompanies the advances of the treatment step by step. "Every single association, every act of the person under treatment must reckon with resistance and represents a compromise between the forces that are striving towards recovery and the opposing ones."[1] Resistance may take many forms, limited only by the organization of the patient's defensive structure. There are countless opportunities for obstructing the therapeutic process. Patients may use a variety of conscious and unconscious methods to carry this out; sessions may be forgotten, intentionally missed, or attended late. The patient may consciously censor material; relevant communications may be avoided through obsessional rumination. The patient may refuse to consider therapist observations and be unwilling to look into the meaning of current behavior and the significance of past experience. Resistance may even take the guise of the patient trying very hard to be a good, conscientious patient. Such patients may dutifully report all thoughts and feelings the therapist seems interested in and sincerely attend to everything the therapist says, while simultaneously avoiding work on real problems, such as the need to please authority figures in order to feel secure. Just about any thought, feeling, or behavior can have a defensive or resistive component.

The resistance may be further understood by considering its relationship to the concept of ego defenses. Ego defenses may be adaptive or maladaptive, conscious or unconscious, used by the patient in daily life or in therapy. Resistance may be thought of as representing the continuing operation and function of the patient's ego defenses as they emerge and are manifest in the therapeutic situation.[2] The compulsive patient, for instance, who uses the defenses of intellectualization and isolation of affect in his everyday life, will likely approach his therapy in a similar manner. Ego defenses used in therapy which impede the therapeutic processes of self-exploration, affect expression, and meaningful interaction with the therapist are termed resistances. The particular form or forms of resistance used by a patient will reflect the defensive organization of the patient's ego.

Patients may resist the therapeutic process and relationship in the same manner in which they obstruct other relationships. Although patients come to therapy asking for, pleading for, or demanding help, they repeatedly have problems forming an alliance in which they can receive it.[3] Patients experience difficulty in developing alliances and working on their concerns because they bring their conflicted means of reacting to and working with people into the patient–therapist interaction. Defenses, both interpersonal and intrapsychic, that impede effective interaction and conflict resolution in the patient's outside life are also enacted in therapy to resist a collaborative therapeutic alliance and an examination of psychological conflict. These behaviors are problematic in that they support the patient's present mode of adaptation and maintain outdated, self-defeating strategies of relating to self and others.

WHY THE PATIENT RESISTS

However much the patient professes to seek change, growth, and conflict resolution, the therapist must posit that a significant portion of his psyche has an investment in the status quo. What fuels this resistance? Why does the patient so tenaciously hold on to conflicted and self-defeating intrapsychic and interpersonal patterns? Why does he resist the therapeutic process? The understanding of resistance is complicated by the observation that patients prove to be attached to the very things that seem to cause them much grief and psychic pain. They cling to their problems and often display a strong reluctance to relinquish them. There are a number of sources for this inclination to impede the process of relinquishing that which is seemingly painful.

Resistance is often engendered by a sense of danger or anxiety. Freud posits that the patient resists the therapeutic process to avoid the anxiety related to the uncovering of repressed intrapsychic conflict.[4] This conflict, typically related to ambivalent wishes and feelings toward early significant others would, if remembered, induce anxiety in the patient. The patient may not only resist experiencing the affect associated with the exploration of conflicted wishes but also, and perhaps just as important, the patient may avoid dealing with the frustration that comes with realizing that secret longings may not ever be fulfilled. The therapeutic process may be resisted to avoid having to tolerate the experience of not getting what one wants, wishes for, or feels one deserves — and of having to work at accepting more mature compromises in one's life.

Sullivan posits that the patient resists to avoid loss of security.[5] Resistances have a self-preservative function. Although the patient wishes relief from his neurotic suffering and disability, he does not want to give up the neurosis itself since it represents his attempt to solve a psychological conflict, and as such represents the best level of adaptation he has been able to achieve on his own.[2] Increased awareness and collaboration with the therapist may unconsciously mean having to deal with what the patient has chosen to avoid or deny. However severe the suffering the patient consciously experiences, the therapist must assume that it is less than what he unconsciously anticipates he would feel were he to "get well."[3] Change and collaboration may be resisted because it seems safer to stay the way one is. What is neurotic about resistance is the patient's implied inability to appreciate the fact that the valid premises for survival of yesteryear are not necessarily valid today.[6]

Resistance has been viewed as a clinging to a closed and fixed internal world of objects based on the fear that since we must have parents, bad parents are better than none at all.[7] If we break away, if we begin to question ourselves and the things that we've learned to do in order to survive, we will be out of the frying pan and into the fire. Character traits that function as resistive strategies within therapy are often the result of identification with the parent and function as a means of maintaining a relationship to that significant other. Giving up that behavior means giving up part of oneself, one's roots, one's identity. The status quo provides some modicum of identity and self-integration.

The patient may resist the therapeutic process for yet another reason: understanding can be painful. A patient may resist the therapeutic interchange because as the therapist responds with empathy, a dissonance is created within the patient. This experience is not what was expected.[8] To a patient unable to empathize with himself, the therapist's empathy may be an unwelcome experience. Genuine connection may: (1) stir up hope where defensively none is desired, (2) feel seductive or indebting, (3) increase one's sense of inadequacy and worthlessness by comparison to the therapist (4) feel like permission to go easy on oneself and become self-pitying or (5) stimulate fears that if one reaches out and connects, rejection will occur.[3] Such concerns, conscious or otherwise, propel the patient to increase efforts to induce the therapist to respond to him as others have done in the past.

The patient also may resist the therapeutic process because as one takes an honest look at oneself and one's relationships, it becomes increasingly difficult to continue to externalize and to blame others or the past for one's difficulties. The more one learns about oneself and one's interactions, the more one learns how he is responsible for his own life and how it is led. This assumption of responsibility provokes an anxiety of its own and is a prime factor in patient resistance.

Another reason a patient may resist change and productive collaboration toward change can be termed the environmental impediment. Those individuals who become involved with the patient on a long-term basis often do so because the patient's neurosis meshes well with their own. Interaction with the patient may satisfy rigid neurotic needs of the partner. The partner may have an investment in keeping the patient involved in an interaction pattern that complements his own. Wachtel notes such classic pairings as the know-it-all husband and the take-care-of-me wife; the hostile overbearing wife whose husband's identity is that of an abused martyr; the fearful pair who reassure each other that others' more adventurous lives are superficial; and the busy pair whose mutual fear of sharing and intimacy comfortably mesh.[9]

In sum, resistance may be best thought of as behaviors that

obstruct the therapeutic process of self-exploration and honest interaction with the therapist. They are a means of defending the patient from anxiety and other painful affects. These may be kindled by the process of exploration and uncovering. Therapeutic examination encourages the patient to face himself in a manner that cuts through defenses and takes away his emotional rationalizations. This can be scary, upsetting, and sometimes frustrating. Anxiety may be elicited by one's being progressively forced to interact with the therapist in a more mature, reality-oriented manner. Such interaction threatens the patient's previously learned, albeit neurotic and maladaptive, means of relating.

THERAPIST STANCE TOWARD RESISTANCE

[It] doesn't mean that you shake your finger at the patient and say, "You're resisting!" That's the worst thing you can do . . . The right way is just to point out to the patient how he keeps himself from thinking certain things and feeling certain things, so that he becomes self-conscious and the evasion doesn't work so automatically. That's all. That's the analyst's scalpel. He can't open up his patient's mind and reach in and start tinkering. The only thing he can do is tell the patient, "Look there," and most of the time the patient doesn't look. But sometimes he does, and then his automatic behavior becomes less automatic.

Janet Malcolm, 1981, pp. 72–73

The therapist's attitude toward resistance will greatly influence the patient's willingness to explore this behavior. For many therapists, the term resistance elicits negative reactions. Resistance to some implies an irresponsible patient who is avoiding therapeutic work. Resistance is best thought of as a complex defensive organization that can be helpful or nonhelpful. The therapist is encouraged to view resistance not as opposition to treatment, but as a critical part of the therapy process. An optimal attitude melds alertness, patience, empathy, and curiosity. The therapist must be alert for manifestations of resistance and be prepared to respond to them sooner rather than later. If the therapist waits too long to examine the resistance, the therapist may acclimate to the patient's resistive style of behavior and come to accept the resistance as just being part of the patient.[10]

While it is important to stay alert for how the patient's resistive strategies will play themselves out in the treatment, and to be able to point this out, it is also important that the therapist have patience in regard to the patient's continued usage of these strategies. They will not be given up with one examination. Freud aptly writes that "one must allow the patient time to become more conversant with this resistance with which he has now become acquainted, to work through it, to overcome it."[11]

The contributions of ego psychology and interpersonal theory have enriched the view of resistance. Resistance was initially seen as something to be broken through (i.e., eliminated) in order to understand the unconscious complexes of the mind that were causing conflict. Change was seen to occur through insight into such complexes. Dynamic theory has evolved to a point where the task regarding resistive behaviors is not to eliminate them but to ascertain their role in the patient's life and in the maintenance of problems in living. Resistance may be most productively viewed as behavior to be examined and understood in its own right rather than an obstacle to be removed as a prelude to change.[10] To be worked with most effectively, resistance is not to be viewed as patient opposition to therapy or the therapist, but rather as a natural and crucial aspect of the process of uncovering therapy. The therapist's failure to cultivate such a view of resistance increases the likelihood of an adversarial therapist–patient relationship.

As a focus in therapy, the resistance becomes as important as the material that is resisted. In the resistances, one finds the elements of conflict embedded in the patient's character structure. With obstinate patients, for example, one slowly begins to observe that, rather regularly, they tend to say "no" before they ever say "yes."[12] The therapist should strive to deal with the defense/resistance before taking up that which is being defended against. Analysis of the process of resisting and its implications often yields considerably more therapeutic movement than a focus on underlying content. Schafer stresses that it is an error to try to elicit directly some thought or feeling that one senses is close to being expressed but is being warded off by the patient. In such situations it is more productive for the patient to learn why it is that this thought or feeling is being warded off. "Suppose the [patient] is evidently struggling not to cry: why the struggle? The [therapist] interested in resistant strategies will first want to know the answer to this question, for that answer will do more for the [treatment] than the crying itself."[13] The therapist's task is not to force certain affects or demand certain behaviors from the patient, but rather to help the patient learn about his strategies of reacting to others and to himself.

The therapist does well to avoid an aggressive style when working with resistance. He must not convey the impression of a gadfly who torments the patient's defenses in an unrelenting fashion, or a military commander who seeks to locate, attack, and destroy the defensive outposts of the enemy. The therapist does not attack defenses in an effort to break through, destroy them, and get at repressed feelings. Such an adversarial stance severely compromises the therapeutic alliance. It is unempathic, persecuting, and most often, doomed to failure.

Schafer suggests that the resisting behavior of the patient

should be approached in an affirmative manner—not as resisting or opposing, but as puzzling or unintelligible behavior that requires understanding. The therapist is cautioned not to view this reorientation to resisting as a ploy, or a means to the end of getting the resisting out of the way so that the therapy can proceed. "Thinking of it in this way is incorrect, for not only does it rule out of court an important part of 'the analysis of the ego,' it also comes perilously close to the analyst's unilaterally trying to make something happen. And what right has the analyst to try to do that?"[14] Rather than setting oneself to break through resistances, one should try to elucidate their role in the life that is being studied and, one hopes, beneficially modified in the therapy.

A final thought regarding the therapist attitude and stance toward resistance. It is of critical importance for the therapist to help the patient learn to become responsible for his own therapy, and not to view it as something done to him or for him by the therapist. Bach recommends that the therapist begin with the attitude of permitting and encouraging the patient to treat himself in the therapist's presence, much as one might allow a child to play in his parents' presence, or a student to practice in the presence of his teacher, without criticism or instruction other than the basic rule. The crucial point, according to Bach, is that the patient can only start to reveal his inmost self, to painfully expose himself, and to begin to treat himself, if he feels that the treatment is his rather than the therapist's. "Naturally, this does not eliminate resistances magically, but it may help the patient to take responsibility for them and talk about them rather than making the analyst primarily responsible for ferreting them out."[15]

Chapter Four

Patient Resistance to the Analysis of Transference in the Here and Now

The utmost pressure which we can bring to bear upon the patient in the direction of giving up [the transference] consists in progressively and with ever greater clearness bringing the transference to light which gradually makes it more difficult and a matter of greater conflict for the patient as an adult to play the infantile part that he has to play in the transference.

Franz Alexander, 1925, p. 494

Patient resistance to here-and-now transference analysis is a pivotal issue in psychodynamic psychotherapy. The patient may resist the examination of the transference relationship by: (1) resisting the development and expression of the transference (i.e., resistance to transference awareness), and (2) resisting the analysis and relinquishing of transference (i.e., resistance to transference resolution). In resistance to awareness of transference, the transference is what is resisted, whereas in resistance to resolution of transference, the transference is what does the resisting.[1] Work with the patient's resistance to awareness of transference is intended to make the implicit transference explicit, while work on resistance to the resolution of transference is intended to aid the patient in examining and modifying the already explicit transference. Thus, the therapist has two sequential tasks in working with transference reactions: first, to help the patient attend to and express reactions and perceptions of the therapist as a form of therapeutic interchange; second, to focus on further clarifying, working through, and resolving transference reactions in order to reduce their harmful effect on present and future interactions. In practice, these tasks blend together and are difficult to separate. For the sake of discussion, however, they will be dealt with in sequential fashion. Resistance to transference awareness will be taken up first.

RESISTANCE TO TRANSFERENCE AWARENESS

To analyze transference reactions, it is first necessary for the patient to become aware of possible transferential components of the patient–therapy interaction. To do this the therapist aims to facilitate both the patient's awareness of, and willingness to discuss, his reactions to the therapist. The psychotherapy patient is often resistant to viewing his reaction to the therapy and the therapist as being an important concern of treatment. The patient may deny having feelings about the therapist or may discount their importance. Patients rarely come to therapy expecting their interaction and relationship with the therapist to become an area of exploration. They tend to avoid recognizing that they experience and react to the therapeutic relationship in any way other than in an uncomplicated professional fashion.[2] They resist viewing the therapy as anything but business, and accordingly, resist the necessity of examining their thoughts, feelings, and reactions to the therapist.

Patients may resist identifying and exploring transference by staunchly maintaining that their reactions to the therapist are based solely on the reality of the person of the therapist and that any conflict generated within the therapy is unrelated to a patient's idiosyncratic means of viewing himself and others. A patient may insist that all feelings toward the therapist, both positive and negative, are fully justified or explained by the conventionally viewed therapeutic situation. A reluctance to talk about feelings for instance, may be rationalized by attributing it to the fear of being overheard by others, to the therapist's silence, or to fear of what the therapist would do with the disclosure, as opposed to being related to the patient's suspicious, mistrustful character style—this style being fostered by childhood experiences with an intrusive, paranoid caretaker. The conclusion patients often want to believe is that there simply is no blind repeating of past patterns of relationship to be understood.[3]

The repetition of the relationship pattern is not likely to be immediately fully recognized by the patient. Part of why he is in therapy is precisely because he is not aware of how he brings about the same set of circumstances, of self-defeating interactions, over and over. In this sense, what transpires in the treatment is at first not experienced as being nearly as familiar as it really is.[4]

Resistances to the awareness of transference represent the most pervasive form of resistance in psychotherapy, yet therapists often fail to examine them systematically.[5] Examination of patient resistance to exploring reactions to the therapist is often slighted in clinical practice. Such underemphasis is a significant reason why transference interpretations may lack emotional impact. Interpretation of the transference will have little impact (other than increasing intellectual defenses) if the patient has not been sensitized to the importance and possible meaning of such feelings, and is to some degree willing to consider the possibility of transference. Without proper preparation it is easy for the patient to distort and reject therapist observations regarding their relationship. As a result dynamic therapy is often practiced in a manner in which the preponderance of energy is directed toward the patient's experience outside of treatment, with little focus on the treatment relationship unless rigid resistances to talking about one's life appear. The here and now is minimized, often avoided.

The therapist is advised not only to focus on the nature of the therapeutic interaction, but also on the methods by which the patient resists focus. This may be a difficult part of therapy. Therapist and client fears of a direct, immediate interchange may collude to discourage the examination of their relationship.

WHY THE PATIENT AVOIDS AWARENESS OF TRANSFERENCE

Patients tend to be reluctant to consider how their internal representations of the world influence their perceptions and reactions to the therapist. Even with preparation and encouragement, the therapist will often find that patients resist the concept of transference and the discussion of their personal thoughts, feelings, and reactions to the therapist. This resistance has a number of sources.

The patient may resist a here-and-now discussion of his feelings toward the therapist because it isn't something customarily done in relationships between patients and those from whom they seek professional services. For that matter, here-and-now interchange regarding one's relationship with another tends to be rather foreign in most social discourse. The patient must be educated as to the importance of this work. The uneducated patient may feel that it is impertinent to consider his reaction to the therapist, or his perceptions of the therapist's feelings. In most everyday situations such foci would seem socially inappropriate.

It becomes particularly hard to admit to feelings if they are to be revealed in front of the very person to whom the feelings relate.[6] Transference awareness may be resisted due to fear of direct and personal interchange with the therapist regarding their relationship. Attending to and discussing feelings about the therapist may be avoided because they are a source of embarrassment and shame. For example, affectionate feelings for the therapist may be difficult for the patient to admit or talk about, particularly if the expression of affection is fraught with conflict.

Transference for certain patients stirs up powerful fears of loss of control, of irreversible or unmanageable regression, or of intolerable closeness and dependence on the therapist. Resistance to transference awareness often is related to the threat involved in the emergence of such feelings and the psychological turmoil that may entail. The patient thus avoids awareness because of fear regarding repressed feelings and reemergence of conflict.[7]

Patients may resist recognizing transference feelings because they unconsciously fear the past will be repeated with the therapist.[8] Being receptive to one's transference feelings, opening up oneself to childhood longings and conflicts, makes the patient vulnerable to reexperience the pain involved in early relationships. The patient may defend himself from potential pain by not allowing himself to be open to his full range of reactions.

Some patients may attempt to rationalize the development of transference in order to avoid awareness of its implications. If one becomes aware of what one is doing and why, it is often much more difficult to continue to act in such a fashion.[9]

Other patients resist attention and examination of the patient–therapist relationship because they are unwilling to accept its "as if" nature.[10] They are unable to give up the therapist as a potential gratifier of frustrated childhood wishes. Acceptance of the "as if" nature of the therapy relationship (and subsequent resolution of transference reactions) requires the patient to explore reactions and feelings for the therapist. Such a task requires frustration of the patient's need to have the therapist as a real, need-satisfying object. Setting aside the therapist as a real object creates tension and a sense of aloneness. Patients strongly conflicted around dependency are often unable to tolerate using the therapy relationship as a means to learn about themselves. They want/demand some type of gratification, be it advice, prohibitions, or love.

No patient can totally set aside the therapist as a need

satisfier (nor would that be helpful). However, those patients who demand a more direct and literal form of need satisfaction (e.g., literal love, sympathy, or guidance of their life) are relatively unwilling to tolerate the loss of immediate tension relief in return for accomplishment of longer-term goals (e.g., insight into intrapsychic conflicts, understanding of neurotic coping behaviors). These patients will resist the conceptualization of treatment relationship as a vehicle to be used to learn about their reactions and interactions with people.

HELPING THE PATIENT BECOME MORE AWARE OF TRANSFERENCE: PATIENT PREPARATION

There is enough that is different, atypical, unexpected, and frightening about therapy without the therapist acting in unexpected ways without explaining why.

Steven Levy, 1984, p. 18

Effective work with transference is facilitated by preparing the patient for therapy through educating him as to the method of treatment. Education serves to: (1) convey respect for the patient's capabilities and support of his autonomy, (2) increase the patient's ability to collaborate by acquainting him with the process, and (3) help the patient tolerate the level of frustration and abstinence within the treatment by making the frustration understandable.[11]

Resistance to awareness of transference is initially managed by the therapist's explanation of the patient's responsibilities in therapy. The importance of openness, honesty, and free expression of thoughts and feelings is highlighted. In addition, the therapist emphasizes the crucial patient–therapist dialogue regarding their interaction and relationship. This preparation may take the form of such statements as: "Please speak as openly and freely as possible about what goes on in your mind during our sessions." "You need to talk about whatever occurs to you: what you think about me, how you feel about coming, how you react to things that I say. I'll try to be direct as well. In the process of trying to understand what goes on between us, we'll be able to figure out your problems with others." Such remarks encourage the person to observe the patient–therapist interaction and to present these observations for joint examination.

Patients need to be educated on the importance of discussing their reactions to the interpersonal transactions that occur between patient and therapist. The patient's natural reticence and perhaps discomfort in observing and attempting to understand the nature of their relationship pattern is pointed out and discussed. As discussed earlier, unless the therapist expresses interest in examining the patient–therapist interaction as a means of identifying and resolving the patient's problems, it is highly unlikely that the patient will initiate such work. Patients most often come to therapy concerned with the resolution of a particular problem or problem constellation. The idea of reflecting on how one's problems in living are enacted in their relationship with the therapist may not be initially compelling.

When attempting to help patients work through their resistance to transference awareness the therapist must be continually aware that patients do not naturally and easily engage in a discussion of the here and now. It is new for some and frightening for others, particularly for those who have experienced repeated failure in attempting to talk about and work out a satisfying relationship. A first step is to help patients understand that the here-and-now focus is not synonymous with criticism and conflict.[12] Many patients have problems not with anger or rage, but with closeness and the expression of positive sentiments. Accordingly, it is important to encourage expression of positive feelings as well as critical ones. Patients often have much to learn regarding recognition and expression of a variety of feelings such as assertion, empathy, dependency, attraction, timidity, etc.

A caveat: the patient learns best about therapy when it is initially explained in a brief, straightforward manner with further explication occurring during the actual process. One is cautioned to avoid treating therapy as a didactic process in which the patient resistance may be bypassed through exhortation, persuasion, and moralization. Levy points out that education and coaxing regarding the importance of transference is often not enough; patient fear and reluctance toward recognition and work with transference often must be explored in terms of why and how the patient benefits from resisting transference work.[13]

THERAPIST STANCE

The patient, through both education and interpretation of resistance, must develop an appreciation for the importance of transference. This includes a readiness to attend to, comment on, and further explore this phenomenon. How does the therapist facilitate this? Foremost, the therapist trusts his theory, and views transference work as a vital means of bringing into view the patient's intrapsychic and interpersonal conflicts. Patient resistance to awareness of transference is met by the therapist's curious, investigative attitude. The therapist is alert to the patient's experience and sensitive to his own feelings and impulses in regard to the patient. He is willing to explore and is open to discussion and interchange regarding their relationship. He is curious as to how and why the patient thinks, feels, and reacts to the therapist as he does and attempts to stimulate the curiosity of the patient as well. The therapist questions the patient's viewing of reactions to the therapist as determined by the present interaction and as not having any relationship to habitual modes of perception and attitude.

Therapists often feel they can be inactive regarding transference development, that transference will gradually expand, become more clear, openly avail itself to therapeutic intervention. Gill cautions that such a stance disregards the resistive component of behavior; unless transference is focused on, it will be denied or avoided.[14] Therapist initiative is needed if the patient is going to be able to overcome the obstacles, both personal and social, involved in an effective examination of the therapeutic relationship. This initiative facilitates the patient's attention to the phenomena and increases the patient's conviction as to the viability of the process of treatment.

IDENTIFYING TRANSFERENCE: ALLUSIONS TO TRANSFERENCE

The dynamically oriented therapist seeks to develop latent transferential material into manifest material for investigation. This is often a difficult task. In association with the anxiety accompanying self-exploration, patients may deny having reactions to the therapist and may actively discount their meaningfulness. Resistance to the awareness and identification of transference attitudes inevitably extends to the related cues as well. The disavowal of both cues and attitudes probably repeats the patient's disavowal of how he understood the earlier experiences which are the genetic basis of the transference attitude.[15]

The therapist may assist in identifying transference feelings by carefully listening for how the patient perceives the therapy, the individual session and, most specifically, for references to the person and activities of the therapist. Transference awareness is aided by exploring allusions to transference in statements the patient makes that do not seem manifestly related to the therapy relationship. The patient's narrative of another interaction or relationship may be a symbolic commentary on the here-and-now relationship. Transference feelings may be communicated in various disguised fashions. They may be expressed through displacement; a patient, experiencing the therapist as controlling and domineering, may discuss his feelings regarding a best friend. Discussing the friend allows ventilation and expression of the feelings regarding being controlled but in an indirect, less dangerous fashion. The now-distant friend is, at the moment, less threatening than the present therapist. The following vignette briefly illustrates displacement.

An adolescent female (AB) was being seen in therapy for problems with interpersonal relationships. AB tended to be rather withdrawn, bordering on avoidant. At a point early in treatment the therapist asked her to characterize her relations with friends. AB was initially silent, then tried to discuss how she saw her friendships but finally stopped, stating she didn't have a clue. She then went on to describe an interaction with a schoolmate which she found very difficult because she had had very little prior interaction with the person. At first she tried to carry on a discussion but then withdrew, feeling inadequate. The therapist, listening with their relationship in mind, was able to draw parallels between the described experience and what had occurred between himself and AB. This enabled AB to more clearly express her feelings regarding the difficulties she experienced talking about herself.

Transference feelings also may be expressed through identification; the patient may become critical and demeaning of

himself as a defense and disguised communication of his perception that the therapist is critical and punitive. In this situation,
the patient ascribes an attitude to himself which is unconsciously attributed to the therapist.

Interpretation and discussion of the patient's possible allusions to transference facilitates an unfolding and ever-clearer
expression of it within the therapy. It is helpful for the therapist
to keep in mind that all communications in therapy have some
relevance to the transference relationship. There is considerable
theoretical grounding for this view. Freud writes that when the
patient is told to say whatever comes to mind, his associations
become directed by the purposive ideas inherent in treatment
and that two inherent purposive themes are the patient's neurosis and his relations to the therapist.[16] He further observes
that the patient remains under the influence of the analytic
situation even though he is not directing mental energy toward
this particular subject, and that nothing will occur to him that
does not have some reference to that situation.[17]

Ferenczi encourages the therapist to take the patient's
relation to the therapist "as the cardinal point of the analytic
material" and to view "every dream, every gesture, every para-
praxis, every aggravation or improvement in the condition of
the patient as above all, an expression of transference and
resistance."[18] Similarly, Heimann stresses that whenever a patient talks, the therapist must relate what is said to what it might
mean regarding the patient's feelings toward the therapist.
"Whether the patient talks about a dream or a current incident
or a childhood episode, the analyst's task is to perceive the
dynamic line which links this with the patient's actual motives,
preconscious or unconscious, towards the analyst."[19]

The principle highlighted here is that patient associations
not explicitly related to the transference are likely to have an
implicit meaning for the relationship and that the therapist must

listen to the content with this in mind. When listening, the therapist could ask himself such questions as: What could this mean regarding the state of our relationship? Why is this occurring now? Strupp and Binder succinctly summarize:

> No matter what the patient communicates directly—and even more important—indirectly, it should never be forgotten that the comments are being addressed to the therapist as a significant other. Therefore, the totality of the patient's behavior always contains comments about the therapist and the real or fantasied relationship with the therapist. This realization should be kept in the forefront of the therapist's thinking and guide listening and participation in the patient's life as it is unfolding during each therapy hour.[20]

The following vignette illustrates allusions to the transference and a possible intervention:

A middle-aged elementary school teacher (BT), sought therapy to work on self-assertion. In the eighth session, BT expressed intense anger with his supervising principal, stating that he was insensitive to students and teachers. BT further reported that the principal was quite rigid and overly structured in his work. The therapist was puzzled by the outburst as BT had thus far been rather controlled in his presentation, and had reported satisfaction with his work environment and the supervisory relationship. The therapist was also aware that BT seemed more tense and distant with the therapist during the past two sessions. As BT continued, the therapist noted parallels between BT's description of his supervisor and past comments about the therapist. In the fourth interview, for example, BT had commented on the orderliness of the therapist's office. To expand the patient's awareness of possible therapy-related implications of his anger, the therapist offered observations regarding comments BT had made regarding the therapy as well as his recent behavior change in the sessions. BT was initially resistant to acknowledging possible parallels between his feelings regarding his supervisor and his therapist. However, after ventilation of his feelings proved unsatisfying, BT acknowledged that his feelings extended beyond the person of his supervisor. BT acknowledged that he was increasingly perceiving the therapist as authoritarian, domineering and wanting to control BT. BT revealed that these feelings were minimally present from the first session but became stronger when the therapist made what BT felt was an insensitive remark about BT's relationship with his wife.

The example of BT highlights the importance of the therapist noting concrete behaviors that are suggestive of here-and-now difficulties. The patient's confusing, self-defeating, and interpersonally distancing styles of relating are best focused on as they are concretely manifest in the relationship. The process of identification and illumination of specific behavior patterns fosters therapeutic gain and patient autonomy. While initial work with a transference theme may require substantial confrontation, the ability of a patient to address such themes increases each time the theme is examined. Patients can then work to relate in a more mature and productive manner. The therapist interacts to encourage the patient's awareness and experience of his conflicted ways of relating as well as their consequences.

Identifying and discussing transference feelings must be done with sensitivity. Wording of the therapist's comments is important. While the therapist may feel reasonably certain that the patient's discussion is an allusion to latent transference feelings, telling a patient what really is being discussed will be met with resistance.[21] The latent content is not what the patient really means. The patient really means the manifest content. What the therapist has perhaps discerned is that a motive for the patient's preoccupation with a particular theme or topic lies in its latent meaning for the transference relationship. To say so is very different from saying what the patient really means.[15] A better approach to identifying and clarifying transference feelings would be to begin with such statements as "A possible meaning of what you are saying, insofar as our therapy is concerned, may be . . ." or "An implication of what you are saying for our relationship is. . . ."

Telling a patient what is really meant is incorrect for other reasons. To speak of real meaning disregards the principle of overdetermination.[22] Briefly, this principle suggests that several factors operate concurrently to create a specific reaction or behavior. The content and sequence of patient material during the therapy session is a response to a complex of motives, only one of which pertains to feelings toward the therapist. The fact that the therapist has discerned further meaning, more disturbing meaning, or more carefully disguised meaning, does not justify the claim that the therapist has discovered the ultimate truth that lies behind the world of appearances—the real world. A sounder claim would be that a point has been reached where reality must be formulated in a more subtle and complex manner than before.[3]

PATIENT RESISTANCE TO TRANSFERENCE AWARENESS: FEAR OF IGNORING REAL LIFE CONCERNS

An underlying premise of dynamic psychotherapy is that patients interact in a way that is generally consistent with their characteristic modes of functioning. A problem occurs, however, when the patient resists viewing a focus on the therapeutic interaction as an integral part of the treatment. The patient may feel that the therapist's attempt to examine their here-and-now relationship is done at the expense of the presenting problem. He may react to the therapist's attempts at relating his associations to the here-and-now transference relationship by feeling that the problems in his life that he came to work on are being ignored. He may argue that it makes no sense to examine his relationship with the therapist since it is time-limited and has no future. Yalom offers a possible response when he suggests that no relationship offers a guarantee of permanency; why, therefore, strip the therapeutic relationship of its current reality because it has no future?[23] In general, the patient must be helped to appreciate that psychodynamically oriented treatment, in its most optimal form, is not a method of direct intervention into the patient's life. Rather, patients are given the opportunity to explore and learn about themselves, including the various means by which their thoughts and feelings and reactions play a part in bringing about their problems in living. This learning and understanding is then carried over into their life situation. Gill contends that after initial discomfort with such a therapeutic stance, patients find it a great relief and an encouraging support to their autonomy that the therapist does not tell them how to live.[15] In all cases, the most effective stance is one that stimulates the patient's curiosity regarding current functioning and encourages further exploration.

To emphasize the transference meaning is not to deny or belittle other meanings, but to focus on the one of several meanings of the content that is the most important for the therapeutic process. Avoidance of such a focus runs the risk of an externally directed therapy in which the patient works to solve seemingly unrelated problems without gaining an understanding of the basic underpinnings of these problems. The result is often partial relief from the presenting concern but little change in character structure/organization.

RESISTANCE TO TRANSFERENCE RESOLUTION

Earlier in this chapter it was noted that the patient resists (1) recognizing and identifying transference attitudes (resistance to transference awareness); and (2) examining and giving up these attitudes (resistance to transference resolution). The therapist is first encouraged to help the patient attend to and discuss his reactions to the therapeutic interaction. This is done through education, modeling, and interpretation of the patient's resistance to awareness of these here-and-now transference feelings. Through analysis of the patient's resistance, the transference is encouraged to expand. The patient is more readily able to attend to and discuss his reactions and interactions with the therapist. As the patient is progressively more able to focus on the patient–therapist interaction, therapeutic attention is directed toward understanding, working through, and resolving the transference components of this relationship. Just as anxieties within the patient make recognition of transference difficult, there also is strong reluctance on the patient's part to relinquish his transferential attitudes and behavior. Just as the patient resists development and expression of transference (i.e., resistance to transference awareness) so too will he resist analysis and resolution transference (i.e., resistance to transference resolution).

. Patients may resist transference resolution, the analysis, and modification of their interaction patterns with the therapist, because these patterns represent tried and true means of relating to others. These interaction patterns are intended, consciously or unconsciously, to create and re-create certain relationship patterns that will best meet security needs. Analysis of transference challenges a rather rigid mode of relatedness. In attempting to identify and work through the patient's resistance to change, the therapist may be seen as a potential threat to psychological survival. Since patients (unconsciously) dare not relinquish patterns of reacting and interacting that serve to maintain interpersonal security, they will often intensify defensive efforts (dig in) or substitute others that serve the same purpose. They will tenaciously cling to their view of the world and thus structure their current experience with significant others, particularly the therapist, in accordance with these expectations.[2] This tenacious clinging may be viewed as an expression of the patient's conviction that he has found some way, albeit painful and self-defeating, to minimize anxiety and maintain some semblance of self-esteem, dignity, and life. Such a stance reflects both the patient's disbelief in an alternative way of life and an intense fear that any other approach to living would be self-esteem-shattering.[24] Holding on to transference reactions, resisting transference resolution, may be viewed as the patient's escape from facing himself, the present moment, and his responsibility in bringing it about.

RESISTANCE TO REMEMBERING (AND FACING ONESELF)

Freud wrote that the transference developed by a patient toward the therapist is a form of resistance to the uncovering/remembering of pathogenic unconscious complexes. Transference resists remembering by acting; rather than recall or think about painful, conflicted relationships, they are experienced and acted out with the therapist. "The compulsion to repeat. . . . replaces the impulse to remember."[25]

The patient may resist remembering by insisting that all feelings toward the therapist, positive and negative, are fully justified or explained by the here and now of the therapeutic situation and relationship. An example is the patient who attempts to mask a mistrustful, withholding style of interacting by stating that the therapist is at fault for not asking the appropriate questions or for not disclosing himself. The felt conclusion of the patient is that there simply is no blind repeating of past patterns of relationship to be understood.[3]

Transference is resistance in that the patient unconsciously insists upon acting out the scenarios of his intrapsychic world and simultaneously wants to view these scenarios as being totally consonant with here-and-now reality. It is a resistance to viewing current interpersonal dilemmas as having a historical component. This reluctance to entertain the possibility that one's reactions toward people are to some extent determined by previous learning is a major impediment to interpersonal learning. It can be very difficult to explore the possibility that one plays a role in creating personal problems when one refuses to face what he brings to the relationship in terms of preconditioned attitudes and reactions.

RESISTANCE TO COLLABORATION AND MATURE INTERCHANGE (AND FACING THE PRESENT MOMENT)

Transference behavior may be viewed as resistance to relating to the therapist in a more mature and collaborative but, because of past learning, more anxiety-provoking manner. Rather than face the uncertainty involved with sorting out the here-and-now relationship, the patient enacts past coping strategies to deal with the therapist. Such strategies compromise the ability of patient and therapist to develop a genuine collaboration concerning the patient's problems. One's transferential attitudes may make it difficult for the patient to use therapy to discuss his problems. The patient's projection of criticalness onto the therapist, for instance, may make it difficult to discuss himself for fear of criticism. Freud noted this possibility when he suggested that "if a patient's free associations fail the stoppage can invariably be removed by an assurance that he is being dominated at the moment by an association which is concerned with the doctor himself or with something connected with him."[26]

RESISTANCE TO AUTONOMY (AND FACING RESPONSIBILITY)

The refusal to examine one's transference reactions and to consider alternate ways of behaving with the therapist expresses a resistance to accepting responsibility for how one chooses to think and feel.[24] It is an escape from facing personal conflicts, the role one has in bringing them about, and the anxiety associated with giving up secure, albeit neurotic and self-defeating behavioral patterns. The patient's avoidance of responsibility is often a fundamental concern in treatment. In some cases, it is a central feature. An illustration:

> A patient (NB) presented with depression and pervasive feelings of isolation. Early in treatment NB revealed that a primary motivation for seeking therapy was to learn to cope with people whom she found to be cold, distant, and uncaring. As therapy progressed, the therapist became increasingly aware of how NB's sarcasm and irritability made it difficult to feel very close to or involved with her. An educated, fastidious, and mannerly person, NB freely

pointed out minor defects in the therapist's dress and manner of speaking. She regularly dismissed the therapist's comments and often referred to the unlikelihood that the therapist could actually be of help to her. NB was initially reluctant to engage in exploration of the nature of their relationship. However, this reluctance dissolved as NB began to have the same complaints about the therapist as she did of others (i.e., that they were distant and uncaring). Through careful examination and discussion of the means by which NB and the therapist related to each other, NB was able to see how her style contributed to her feeling isolated and distant. As NB was able to perceive that her approach to people in general was similar to her pattern with her therapist, it became increasingly difficult for her to see others as the sole cause of her painful relationships. Through such work, NB was encouraged to assume responsibility for her role in creating her life situation. This required her to relinquish externalizing, projective defenses, as well as whatever security (although maladaptive) they furnished.

As therapy progresses, the patient increasingly learns how he is responsible for and creates his own life. Such knowledge engenders a myriad of feelings, including hope (I constructed my world, I may be able to change it); anxiety (I have more control than I thought and I'm not sure I can cope with it); ego-deflation (I can't blame others for my problems any more); and often sadness (since I'm responsible for my life, I may have to relinquish my childhood wish of nurturance and care without work or reciprocation).[23]

Part III

Therapist-Centered Resistance

Chapter Five

Therapist Resistance to Analysis of Transference in the Here and Now

The therapist's inability and/or unwillingness to deal with the transference is probably the most common reason for the failure of psychotherapy—the cause of its becoming a boring, circular, repetitive recounting of symptoms, with emphasis on placing the blame for them on external situations, past and present.

Michael Basch, 1980, p. 40

When surveying the history of psychodynamic technique, considerable rationale may be found for an active focus on the understanding and working through of the here-and-now transference relationship between patient and therapist. In 1912 Freud stressed work with transference as the vehicle of cure.[1] Transference was seen as playing the central role of bringing to life hidden conflict and furnishing an arena to work it through. In 1925 Rank and Ferenczi, in their classic work on analytic technique, placed great importance on the reliving of maladaptive patterns in relation to the therapist and of recognizing their inappropriateness.[2] Shortly thereafter, Strachey also stressed the importance of the here-and-now focus. He wrote,

> Instead of having to deal as best as we may with conflicts of the remote past, which are concerned with dead circumstances and mummified personalities, whose outcome is already determined, we find ourselves involved in an actual and immediate situation, in which we and the patient are the principal characters and the development of which is to some extent at least under control.[3]

More recently, Bion wrote that "psychoanalytic observation is concerned neither with what has happened nor with what is going to happen, but what is happening."[4]

Despite the attention given to understanding and resolving the transference in the here and now, such work is often underemphasized. What might account for this? Wachtel notes that Freud appeared more interested in what the here-and-now transference relationship meant regarding the past than its function in the patient's present life.[5] Gill posits that Freud's case histories, because they focus on the results of the analysis rather than the details of the process, are perhaps misconstrued as emphasizing work outside the transference much more than work with the transference.[6] He further suggests that the analytic community is reluctant to emphasize the role of analysis of the transference in the here and now because it endangers the role of insight, and argues for interpersonal influence and cure by suggestion as the significant factors in change.[7]

Lipton argues that analysts deemphasized interpersonal experience in psychotherapy because of fear that it opened the way to such techniques as Alexander's manipulation of the transference to create a corrective emotional experience.[8] Alexander postulated that an interpersonal experience with the therapist would facilitate correct or faulty attitudes learned with early caretakers. To facilitate this experience he suggested the therapist actively seek to encourage certain transference reactions and that he enact certain curative roles with the patient (e.g., nonjudgmental father). Alexander's work created a stirring among contemporary analysts. His suggestions were viewed as overly controlling and manipulative. A late 1940s–early 1950s movement in analytic technique toward greater neutrality and more strict use of interpretation was seen in part as a reaction to Alexander's suggestion to engineer specific types of transference relationships in order to allow a relearning by the patient.

In addition to the above-mentioned theoretical rationale for avoiding here-and-now work, the actual experience of the therapist in therapy may facilitate its avoidance. Here-and-now work contains the potential to involve *both* patient and therapist in affect-laden and potentially disturbing interchanges. *Both* patient and therapist may be reluctant to acknowledge and work with certain aspects of their relationship. *Both* participants may be motivated to escape such interactions due to the anxiety these interactions are sensed to engender. A mutual conspiracy may develop between therapist and patient to avoid focus on their relationship, and the anxiety and discomfort involved in such a focus. The result is often an experience-distant, intellectualized understanding of patient problems. This superficial insight is achieved at the expense of genuine emotional involvement and the fundamental change that such involvement may offer.

Not only will patients resist working on here-and-now transference issues, therapists as well must be aware of their own resistances to here-and-now work. The motivations underlying these resistive behaviors are complex but most often relate to therapist discomfort with the affects generated in a here-and-now examination of the patient–therapist relationship. The nature of these motivations will be taken up at this point.

AVOIDANCE OF THE INTENSITY OF HERE-AND-NOW AFFECT

> *No one who, like me, conjures up the most evil of those half-tamed demons that inhabit the human breast, and seeks to wrestle with them can expect to come through the struggle unscathed.*
>
> Sigmund Freud 1905, p. 109

It has been contended that the therapist's faint-heartedness in discussing transference manifestation is responsible for more stagnation in dynamic therapy than any other attitude.[9] The therapist may resist here-and-now work to avoid the affect which such a stance may unlock. Fears associated with a direct, immediate interchange are often strong enough to encourage its avoidance. It is often more comfortable for the therapist to make a genetic interpretation or to avoid relationship issues entirely by maintaining a focus on external, content-oriented (as opposed to transference) problems. As a result, immediate difficulties between patient and therapist are avoided. "By being concerned . . . with . . . 'outside' reality, a defense against something immediate is provided."[10]

Strachey describes a special difficulty the therapist must overcome in order to make direct and mutative interpretations regarding the patient–therapist relationship. This difficulty concerns the therapist's unconscious perception that such here-and-now comments would expose the therapist to a danger. Therapist resistance may be rationalized into the difficulty of deciding whether or not the particular moment has come to make a comment on the relationship. The therapist may decide, for instance, that the patient needs more time to increase trust in the therapist before anxiety-provoking issues are examined. But behind this, Strachey suggests there lurks a fear of actually making a here-and-now transference interpretation, for there seems to be a constant temptation for the therapist to do something else instead, to ask questions, give advice or direction, to provide theoretical input or perhaps extratransference interpretations.

> All of this strongly suggests that the giving of a mutative interpretation is a crucial act for the analyst as well as for the patient, and that he is exposing himself to some great danger in doing so. And this in turn will become intelligible when we reflect that at the moment of interpretation the analyst is in fact deliberately evoking a quantity of the patient's id-energy while it is alive and actual and unambiguous and aimed directly at himself.[11]

The patient's willingness to work with transference is intimately related to the therapist's comfort with such work. The patient quickly picks up therapist anxiety. The patient must feel that the therapist can take aggressions or seductions—otherwise they won't be shared.[12] Discomfort on the part of the therapist in dealing with here-and-now affect conveys fear of those feelings and implicit encouragement of their suppression/repression, which increases the potential for their acting out and/or displacement onto other objects.

DISCOMFORT WITH PATIENT SCRUTINY

By asking patients to explore their feelings regarding the therapeutic relationship, and by commenting on this relationship, the therapist faces the potential discomfort and anxiety of offering himself as a target for feelings, fantasies, and perceptions that may threaten his own self-esteem and self-image.[13] A patient's perception of the therapist may be insightful and penetrating. Therapists who can't tolerate close scrutiny of themselves may find here-and-now work difficult, especially when the patient chances upon real foibles. The therapist may have a hard time listening to things that wound his ego. Such apprehension may impede investigating areas of potential conflict between patient and therapist, or perhaps lead to the therapist's investigating in a manner that controls or forecloses the patient's reaction. The phrase *countertransference resistance* has been used to refer to this difficulty the therapist has with investigating in a manner that will assist the patient to say everything.[14]

THERAPIST AS THE CENTER OF CONFLICT

There is another quality of here-and-now work that may promote therapist resistance. Willingness of the therapist to foster and work with transference reaction moves the therapist into an active involvement in the central crunch of the patient's conflict with self and others.[15] Involvement of the therapist in the repetition of a patient's intrapsychic and interpersonal struggle is a potent experience. Glover contends that "at no stage of an analysis are the analyst's reactions, or his convictions about the fundamental truths of psychoanalysis, put to a more severe test than during that stage when the ground of the patient's conflict has been shifted, from external situations or internal mal-adaptations of a symptomatic sort, to the analytic situation itself."[16]

In psychodynamically oriented treatment, the therapy is framed in a manner that encourages the development of transference feelings. These strong, compelling, often puzzling feelings are then sifted through, discussed, analyzed, and put in perspective. Being directed toward the therapist, they are readily available for work. This involvement with the patient's struggles, given the patient's attempt through projective identification to externalize his inner world of objects, places great pressure on the therapist's ability to contain and hold the patient's introjects. This is often much more taxing than when the topic of examination is the past, or an outside experience. The wear and tear involved in the experience of analyzing and working through here-and-now conflict is considerable and is a major reason therapists may resist transference work.

THERAPIST DEFENSES

We can hardly be surprised if constant pre-occupation with all the repressed impulses which struggle for freedom in the human psyche sometimes causes all the instinctual demands which have hitherto been restrained to be violently awakened in the analyst himself.

Sigmund Freud, 1937, p. 402

Therapists may resist here-and-now work due to the strain it places on their defensive structure. The extent to which such work is undertaken often relates to the therapist's ability to tolerate the affect elicited by an immediate, here-and-now interchange with the patient. Here-and-now affect may be resisted by the therapist due to underlying fear regarding the neutralization and subsequent control of his own erotic and aggressive impulses. The increase in affect involved in here-and-now processing may stimulate the therapist's personal areas of conflict and become problematic if the therapist has not learned to constructively manage conflicts. This is especially true when working with patients presenting more seriously conflicted interpersonal relationships. Interacting with such individuals places an intense pressure on the adaptive defenses of the therapist that may result in ego regression and the acting out of conflict by the therapist that had previously been mastered and modified.[17] The therapist's constructive means of dealing with such conflicts may be sorely tested as the therapist attempts to discuss and work through an especially difficult impasse with the patient. In such cases, a therapist may unwittingly attempt to escape the intense pressure placed on his adaptive defenses by shifting attention from the heat of the immediate situation to an exploration of past relationships.

It is often more comfortable for the therapist to make a genetic connection than to focus on the here-and-now manifestations of transference. Flight away from the transference and to the past can be a relief to both patient and therapist.[6] The therapist may seek affective distance and proper rapport to spare himself the stimulation of intense transference.[12] Such strategy, while quieting things down for the moment, generally complicates the working through of transference material.

THERAPIST CONFIDENCE

Therapists may resist here-and-now work because they are not sure they can help. Their willingness to comment on the nature of the patient's in-session behavior, and to explore this within the confines of the patient–therapist interaction, communicates a willingness to deepen the relationship and to assume some responsibility for its ultimate well-being. This requires the therapist to have some measure of confidence in his ability to effect change in the manner in which patient and therapist relate to each other. An underlying belief, for instance, in the inherent rigidity of character structure may prompt the therapist to provide more support, advice, and encouragement than an analysis of transference behavior. In a related vein, the therapist may believe in the potential for interpersonal change but be disillusioned regarding his personal ability to effect change in his personal relationships. This feeling may generalize to his relationship with the patient, with the preponderance of energy being focused away from here and now toward outside or past events—the message being "I may not be able to help you feel differently in our relationship, but maybe I can help you with other relationships in your life."

A here-and-now focus communicates interest in interacting closely, the possibility of improving the interaction, as well as some sense that the therapist can facilitate this improvement. If the therapist feels unsure or inadequate regarding this task (or if the therapist gains gratification or is most comfortable with the present interaction pattern), he may decline a here-and-now focus. To deal directly with the patient's resistive strategies sets up an opportunity for failure to elicit change. Any doubts in the therapist regarding ability to elicit change are magnified in a situation in which the therapist grapples with a patient's adaptive and defensive style in their own relationship.

An additional concern that may be voiced by the therapist in support of avoiding here-and-now work is that such a focus will be viewed by the patient in a seductive fashion and will be misunderstood or misinterpreted. This stance is most often the result of the therapist's tendency to take a social versus asocial approach to therapy relationship.[18] Whereas in normal social interchange a probing investigation of one's feelings, attitudes, and reactions toward the other may be viewed as out of place, perhaps intimidating, perhaps overstimulating, in therapy such an examination is a critical part of the change process. The therapy relationship may be productively viewed as a microcosm of one's other relationships and, in the safe havens of objectivity, empathy, and neutrality, the patient is offered the opportunity for in-depth understanding and the practicing of new ways of reacting and interacting.

AVOIDANCE OF NEGATIVE AFFECT

There is no way the analyst can avoid being hated. . . . To begin with, the analyst will be hated for daring to try to understand and formulate anything at all about the analysand, for any such activity threatens the status quo and is experienced as an attack.

Roy Schafer, 1983 p. 155

The therapist's discomfort and unwillingness to tolerate the patient's expressions of negative affect* may lead to an avoidance of a here-and-now focus. Inability of the therapist to bear the direct experience of patient hostility, anger, and demanding

---

*Negative affect is defined as representing such emotions as anger, hostility, demandingness, frustration, and disappointment. It is not used in a pejorative fashion as if to say that such emotions are bad, unacceptable, and should be eliminated from the therapeutic hour.

ness is a common clinical problem. Unresolved negative transference feelings, often stemming from the therapist's inability to effectively analyze the patient's hostile reaction to the therapy, are a common precipitant of premature termination and the source of many stalemated therapies.[15] Although there is no way the therapist can avoid being a target of the patient's negative feelings, there are many ways to provoke unanalyzable hostile reactions, or to duck the issue and instead help the patient to continue to repress it.[12] Therapists with problems tolerating negative affect slowly accumulate a caseload of primarily grateful patients. Such therapists often provide excessive support and overt nurturance. They may be unusually available by phone or extra appointment. They rarely point out the patient's aggressiveness/hostility and often engage in actions that make it difficult for the patient to experience anger.[19] Intent on avoiding negative affect and keeping the interaction on a positive note, an overly gratifying relationship is unconsciously/consciously fostered. Such gratification drives negative affect underground through suppression or repression and often leads to its displacement onto other objects.

SOURCES OF NEGATIVE AFFECT

The therapist working in the here and now must be prepared to deal with the patient's negative affect, which may come from a variety of sources.

1. The patient may have long-repressed rage resulting from faulty responses to early crises.[20] Patient hostility may be a reaction to shortcomings of unempathic or hostile adults displaced to the therapist. The patient may interpret the

therapy in a manner similar to the painful experiences with others and react with hostility.

2. The patient may be reacting to actual failures by the therapist. Deficiencies in training and supervision or countertransference concerns may result in an inability of the therapist to accurately understand and empathically attune himself to patient needs.

3. The patient may react with hostility because here-and-now work directly focuses on the patient's defenses and resistive strategies. Such work may elicit anger as the therapist strives to have the patient deal with material that is being avoided. As the patient's means of maintaining security — his view of self, others, and the world — is challenged, a hostile (defensive) reaction may result.

4. Negative affect (disappointment, frustration) may also result when the patient's wish for relief from his suffering is not met quickly enough, or in the manner expected. Patients enter treatment with the idea, often preconscious, that if they tell the therapist their problems and do what the therapist directs, they will be cured. Passive–receptive longings for an omnipotent parental object who solves the problems of life exist in most everyone and are especially stimulated by the structure of the doctor–patient relationship. These longings are most often unsatisfied, resulting in disappointment and frustration with the therapist.

5. Yet another source of patient frustration has to do with the therapist's attempt to avoid becoming overly engaged in the patient's neurotic interpersonal scenarios. A major source of frustration for the patient is the therapist's unwillingness to react as he is expected to on the basis of the patient's internal programming.[21] The expected reaction reassures the patient that his particular strategies, albeit self-defeating, will enable him to predict and control his

environment. This inability to evoke the anticipated, though often painful, response often elicits great anxiety and then frustration and anger from the patient.

Therapists may be reluctant to examine negative affect due to fear that a potentially difficult and upsetting interaction may interfere with the development of the therapeutic alliance. It is likely that the opposite is often a better reflection of reality. Inability of the therapist to confront troublesome aspects of the therapeutic interaction most often results in the development of therapeutic impasse. Unless manifestations of the hostile, mistrustful components of transference are confronted early in treatment, there is little development of a therapeutic alliance.[17] Without a focus on what impedes the patient–therapist collaboration, treatment is at the mercy of the maladaptive and self-defeating ways in which the patient typically reacts. Avoidance of such issues results in a problem-solving, externally directed (as opposed to intrapsychically directed) treatment; such a treatment aids in problem resolution but often effects little personality change. A generalizable coping strategy for similar problems is not learned.

Even though patients may resist, they look to the therapist for expert guidance to enable them to overcome their difficulties. The inability of the therapist to discuss the patient's negative reactions may convey the message that the therapist is not competent or too frightened to work with such material. The patient may comply with this communication by avoiding such feelings, resulting in a superficial treatment. He may also flee, withdraw, or become more provocative.[22] And at a deeper level, the patient's fear of his, and others', aggression is validated.

If any one element is underestimated in approaching a career as a psychotherapist, it is the amount of hostility and rejection that will be one's lot in the pursuit of therapeutic helpfulness. A great threat to personal integrity and self-worth will come about through open rejection of one's most heartfelt efforts to be of use, the sharing of intuitions with the patient, and the provision of great patience and forbearance; the patient may still, in spite of all these, declare the therapist inadequate, short of the mark, and uncaring.

Sheldon Roth, 1987, pp. 1–2

AVOIDANCE OF THERAPIST COUNTERTRANSFERENCE

There exists in most of us a tendency to avoid or deny countertransference feelings. This is based on several factors. Primarily, it is due to the nature of the impulses themselves. What we repress in relation to our patients are the same incestuous, perverse, envious and vengeful desires that we prefer to not see in ourselves in any case. But also this denial is tolerated because it accords with certain highly unrealistic but socially accepted images of what a psychotherapist is or should be — calm, without anger or desire, mature, only a little neurotic. . . .

Winslow Hunt and Amnou Issacharoff, 1977, pp. 100–101

Countertransference refers to the therapist's emotional reactions to the patient developed during the treatment process. Such reactions stem from unresolved conflicts of the therapist and/or the impact on the therapist of the patient–therapist interaction, especially the patient's conflicted interpersonal strategies. During the early development of dynamic theory, countertransference reactions were seen as detrimental to analyst neutrality; for that reason, they needed to be guarded against. Freud himself observed that there were many things he did not want his patients to say to him.[14] He found that he wanted to avoid the feelings he felt when a patient, in a state of strong negative or erotic transference, aroused complementary feelings in him. Arousal of such feelings, and the subsequent defenses to these feelings, were viewed as compromising his ability to work freely with the patient.

As dynamic theory evolved, increased attention was given to the interpersonal and interactional component of the patient–therapist relationship. The therapist began to be viewed not only as a neutral figure, but as a barometer of the interpersonal and intrapsychic mechanisms of the patient. A greater acceptance has evolved in the use of countertransference reactions to understand the patient's conflicted interpersonal strategies.

Constructive management of countertransference places strong demands on the therapist's adaptive and defensive operations. The therapist must be able to use his emotional reactions to the patient to ascertain the organization of the patient's internalized self and object relations. His reactions are indicators of what it's like to be with this person, what roles the person scripts others into, and how the person typically feels about himself. These feelings must not be foreclosed. The therapist who is unable to accept his thoughts or feelings toward the patient runs the risk of denying them or discharging them. In the service of denial, the therapist may unwittingly discourage any future interactions that threaten to provoke the unacceptable countertransference response. The patient may respond with triumph or fear to the therapist's efforts to close off an area of investigation, either pursuing the topic with more vigor—thus creating a vicious cycle—or relinquishing any hope of mastery and thus withdrawing.[22] The therapist who is unable to tolerate and contain his feelings toward the patient may also discharge them through acting out. In such situations the therapist may enact the disavowed, rationalizing this behavior in terms of "pathology" of the patient. The therapist, for instance, who is unable to tolerate his anger with a patient may administer a reprimand and attribute this response to the provocativeness of the patient.

The presence of countertransference does not imply that the therapist is an immoral person or an inadequate clinician. As dynamic theory has evolved, therapists have realized that attempting to eliminate countertransference was not only impossible but also unproductive for there is much to be learned about a patient by means of analyzing one's personal reaction to him. What is crucial is for countertransference to be explored and understood in order to increase the therapist's ability to intervene in a helpful manner.

Although clinical theory has found excellent use for countertransference reactions, they are still often regarded with a certain degree of anxiety by the practicing therapist. Tower remarks that the therapist's resistance to awareness of countertransference is often greater and more insidious than the patient's resistance to becoming aware of his transference reactions.[23] Racker notes that the therapist will tend to avoid his countertransference when such reactions would be rejected by his ego or superego ideal. The therapist may foreclose awareness of certain feelings if these feelings are dissonant to the way he wants to view himself.[24] Similarly, Issacharoff notes that therapists have basic and profound resistances to becoming an observer of their countertransference and require a constant reawakening.[25]

Though countertransference is no longer seen as totally belonging in the realm of therapist neurosis, there still remains considerable resistance to its identification and analysis. Difficulties in discussing countertransference are often due to attributing it to personal difficulties versus a response to the patient–therapist interaction. It may be hard to focus in that it may seem to reflect on the therapist's character (e.g., sexual feelings make him a lecher). In addition, openness to what the patient stirs up may be overstimulating and may increase the therapist's wish to act out. If it is repressed, the temptation to act is lessened.

These considerations regarding countertransference are of considerable importance in here-and-now work. The intensive, interactional give-and-take, and the high level of emotional involvement that characterizes this focus, offer a fertile soil for the emergence of a host of feelings and reactions to the patient. The therapist may deemphasize the here and now to avoid the surfacing of these reactions.

You can exert no influence if you are not susceptible to influence.
Carl Jung, 1933, p. 49

MANIFESTATIONS OF THERAPIST RESISTANCE

Anxieties inherent in here-and-now transference analysis may lead the therapist to resist this aspect of the treatment process. Therapist resistance may be manifested in myriad fashions. There are numerous means by which a therapist may obstruct here-and-now work. They include: (1) an overemphasis of genetic investigation, (2) limited therapist activity, (3) overreliance on the positive transference, (4) failure to differentiate transference from nontransference behavior, (5) presentation of a posture of certainty when interpreting, and (6) premature interpretation of patient projections. These will be explored in subsequent chapters.

Chapter Six

Overemphasis of Genetic Interpretation

The tactical goal of elaboration of earlier life experience is important only if this new understanding of past events and conflicts ultimately results in more effective interaction and adaptation to conflict and stress in the present.

Paul Dewald, 1964, p. 239

The therapist may resist the analysis of transference in the here and now by means of an overemphasis on the genetic determinants of the patient's present problems in living. The past may be concentrated on to resist exploration of the present moment. Discussion of past events to the exclusion of current here-and-now affect may result in an intellectualized discussion that lays blame for difficulties on how the patient was treated as a child. The reflex-like focus on the past has numerous complications. The therapist who is prone to continually relate a here-and-now interchange to the past also conveys to the patient that the therapist's feelings are vulnerable and must be protected. In such situations the patient may be subtly encouraged to displace legitimate feelings for the therapist to early caretakers. Such a stance is problematic for therapy in that it reinforces the defenses of externalization and projection and makes responsibility assumption more difficult.

Overemphasis on the past and on genetic reconstruction, particularly early on in therapy, poses another problem. Even with extensive therapy, patients recall only minute portions of their past experience. Recall of the past is an active reconstruction heavily influenced by the patient's current psychology. Patients tend to selectively recall and synthesize the past so as to achieve a consistency with the present view of self.[1] How a patient represents his past tells us how he needs to see that past now. History may be altered to suit the current emotional state. At best his account is only fairly well correlated with the actual past. It is by no means identical with it.[2]

Since the information patients provide regarding parents and childhood is often distorted, early genetic interpretations and reconstructions based on such information are often inaccurate and premature. In response to this, Reppen suggests that when reconstructing past events, the therapist emphasize *how* the patient experienced the event rather than *what* actually occurred.[3] The quality and symbolic meaning of the experience may not be the same as the event in which the person participated.[4] Experiences are integrated differently depending on the developmental level of the person at the time of the experience and the type of relationship the individual had with those involved in the experience. Thus, the therapist cannot assume but needs to explore what a particular event meant and how it was experienced by the patient.

> [This] internal world of object representations as seen in conscious, preconscious, and unconscious fantasies never reproduces the actual world of real people with whom the individual has established relationships in the past; it is at most an approximation, always strongly influenced by the very early object-images of introjections and identifications.
>
> Otto Kernberg, 1976, p. 33

VALUE OF GENETIC INVESTIGATION

Although analysis of transference in the here and now emphasizes use of the immediate patient–therapist relationship to learn about and resolve conflictual patterns of interaction, this should not be misconstrued as negating the importance of understanding the patient's developmental history. Attention to the development of conflictual patterns offers the patient a chance to understand and to connect across time the events of his life. This helps build a sense of self-history and aids in consolidation of identity. It also promotes confidence that troubling feelings may be understood, and one is not involved in a confused meandering through unrelated situations. In addition, Sullivan points out that finding out how things start often provides a great deal of information as to what they represent, whereas their more sophisticated, more mature manifestations may be very obscure.[5]

A further value in examining one's history is that as the past is explored and reexplored, one is often able to reintegrate his view of it. Relationships with early significant others may come to be understood in a somewhat different and perhaps more complex manner; one may even develop some empathy for those individuals formally perceived through the eyes of the frightened child. A new view of the past may affect the patient's view of himself.[6] A patient, for instance, may come to the realization that while not optimally responded to as a child, it was not because he was unloved, but rather because the parent was harried, overextended, and facing formidable obstacles to effective parenthood. Such a realization may allow the patient to reevaluate his self-worth and loveableness, which formerly was based on feeling unattended to and ignored while growing up.

At certain junctures in the therapy, exploration of historical data may offer patient and therapist needed distance from a present interaction that is particularly conflictual. A present impasse may be momentarily defused by focus on the details of similar experiences in the patient's history. This often helps to free the patient and the therapist from the necessity of immediately understanding whatever is going on in the here and now.

This may be returned to at a later point. Such techniques may be particularly important when working with the patient who is more fragile and panic-prone. Such patients' anxiety tends to mushroom and swamp them. An interpretation at the height of an affective conflict may overwhelm the patient, as opposed to providing him a better understanding of himself. The therapist may choose not to deal with the conflict at the hot moment but rather he may be back to it in a later session, when the conflict is not so intensely active. Pine terms this intervention "striking while the iron is cold."[7]

A focus on genetic investigation is of additional value in that it provides a shared focus for discussion and collaboration while patient and therapist get used to and become comfortable with each other. Certain patients are initially unable to manage the anxiety engendered by more direct interchange. Discussion of past events may increase comfort and security, which enables a more interpersonal focus to develop.

Knowledge of the past facilitates the therapist's relationship with the patient in another important manner: in-depth understanding of the early development of a particular interpersonal stance enhances the possibility of empathy and meaningful relationship. Knowledge of another's process of becoming is often indispensable to knowing the person.[8] For example, a man with an abrasive, hostile manner may become understandable once the therapist learns of his suffering at the hands of a sadistic parent. Understanding of a patient's development thus enhances the therapist's ability to feel for, and with, the patient, allowing a deepening of the present interaction.

OPTIMAL USE OF GENETIC INTERPRETATION

Once upon a time it seemed obvious that you could best understand how things are by asking how they got to be that way. Now attention [is] directed to how things are in all their immediate complexity.

Frank Kermode, 1987, p. 3

Psychoanalytic work has often been understood as examining the present as a way of throwing light upon the repressed past. Sorting out of the past from the present, the imagined from the actual, is of utmost helpfulness. What is most important, however, is the accent. The *primary* value of exploration of genetic material is to facilitate the understanding and progressive modification of the present relationship. Understanding the past is used to decrease its harmful effects on the present. The therapist makes excursions into historical research in order to understand something which is interfering with present communication with the patient in the same way that a translator might turn to history to elucidate an obscure text.[9] Fortified with knowledge of the patient's development and of his relationships with early significant others, the therapist is better positioned to understand his own reactions to him. Kernberg and colleagues suggest this may be done by imagining scenarios involving the patient and significant others until one of the players can be understood to fit the therapist's here-and-now experience with the patient. Repetitive efforts of this kind gradually lead to an emerging picture of the patient's internal world of self and object representations in all their contradictory aspects.[10]

When working with the interplay of past and present both patient and therapist must keep in mind that what has happened in earlier life, in childhood or infancy, is not in and of itself crucial in psychotherapy. Of far greater significance is the manner in which events that occurred during a person's development determine, modify, or restrict his adjustment in present situations and in his present life experience.[11] The crucial task is not to uncover the past but to use this knowledge for the assistance it can offer in more deeply grasping the meaning of present functioning. The past is used to make sense of the present.

Alexander and French caution that memory material must always be correlated with the present life situation, and the patient must never be allowed to forget that he came for help in solving actual life problems, not for an academic understanding of the etiology of his condition.[12] Though understanding of the past may be used to decrease its harmful effects on the present, the therapist must keep in mind that change rests on the reliving and modification of meaningful patterns within the therapeutic interaction and not on the elucidation of past events.[13]

Here-and-now work makes one's past more intelligible. A sense of continuity and coherency is often attained. In fact, effective here-and-now work often leads to a recovery of past memories; this is in accord with Freud's observation that memories of the past often appear after resistance—in this case, transference resistance—is worked through.[14]

Wachtel offers additional insight to the function of the past in the development and maintenance of psychological conflict. Taking a stance that emphasizes the role of present behavior in generating maladaptive patterns, Wachtel argues that while a patient's problems may indeed have their *origin* in early childhood, the effective causes today stem from his *present* interactions with others (and in the meaning such interactions have for the person and the new fantasies and wishes generated as a consequence). Wachtel writes,

> If one looks closely at an instance of persisting psychological conflict, it is usually possible to see how the desires and conflicts which dominate the persons's life can be understood as *following from*, as well as *causing*, the way he or she lives that life. By resisting the temptation to explain the longing or fantasy quickly

as a simple perpetuation of the past, we may see how it is brought about in the present, both by the patient's own behavior and by the behavior he evokes in others.[15]

For Wachtel, the heart of the psychodynamic process is not in the patient's preserved past but in the vicious cycles that past events set in motion, and that are maintained by the complications resulting from current interaction patterns.

One does not readily give up a love or a hatred, personal or national, only because one learns that it is based on a crushing defeat of the remote past.

Leo Stone, 1973, p. 51

Chapter Seven

Constricted Therapist Activity

Lack of emotional responsiveness, silence, the pretense of being an inhuman computer-like machine which gathers data and emits interpretations do no more supply the psychological milieu for the most undistorted delineation of the normal and abnormal features of a person's psychological makeup than do an oxygen-free atmosphere and a temperature close to the zero-point supply the physical milieu for the most accurate measurement of his physiological responses. Appropriate neutrality in the analytic situation is provided by average conditions. The analyst's behavior vis-à-vis his patient should be the expected average one — i.e., the behavior of a psychologically perceptive person vis-à-vis someone who is suffering and has entrusted himself to him for help.

Heinz Kohut, 1977, p. 253

Here-and-now analysis of transference is facilitated by an active, give-and-take dialogue in which the therapist seeks to identify, examine, and modify neurotic patterns currently being enacted within the treatment hour. The therapist may resist/obstruct this analysis by severely limiting his activity level vis-à-vis the patient. Such behavior often reflects theoretical and/or countertransference errors in regard to the therapeutic concept of neutrality.

VALUE OF ACTIVITY

A more active intervention style, greater risk-taking behavior, and more willingness to focus on the interaction are inherent to here-and-now work. Resistance to transference and transference itself are examined in a more active manner than in traditional dynamic therapy. Through active involvement with resistance and transference, the therapist strives to create a level of therapeutic tension that involves greater levels of affect and emotional engagement than is typically experienced in the therapy session.

An active approach to transference analysis has other

advantages. An active give-and-take with the patient is invaluable in that it affords the therapist an opportunity to clarify more fully the meaning of the patient's statements. Often through the therapist's efforts to understand, the patient's understanding of himself is furthered. Sullivan notes that few things do the patient more good than care on the part of the therapist to discover exactly what the patient means. "Almost every time one asks, 'Well, do you mean so and so?' the patient is a little clearer on what he does mean."[1] Whenever the therapist's attempt to discover what the patient is talking about leads the patient to be somewhat more clear on what he is thinking about or attempting to communicate, his grasp of living, according to Sullivan, is to some extent enhanced. "And no one has grave difficulties in living if he has a good grasp on what is happening to him."[2]

An active, energetic dialogue is often necessary for the therapist to gain a detailed understanding of just what led up to what in the patient's life, particularly in the here-and-now interaction. Knowledge of the transference relationship is enriched by a detailed inquiry of the sequences in the patient's interaction with the therapist. Just as the therapist must actively seek to understand the patient, it is also necessary that the patient understand what the therapist means. The patient's understanding does not always follow the therapist's single statements, even if the therapist always expressed himself with ideal clarity, which in fact he does not. Here, too, some conversation becomes necessary.[3]

A vigorous focus on the patient–therapist interaction often allows more rapid identification of the patient's problems in living than a more traditional, wait-and-see stance. The rapid identification of emotional conflict, and demonstration of how it manifests interpersonally within the therapy, allows the working-through process to begin earlier. This crucial process of unlearning and relearning, accomplished by repetitively experiencing and studying one's problems from different angles and perspectives, is facilitated by the therapist's active involvement in the examination of the transference component of the therapeutic interaction.

The therapist may assume an overly constricted, passive, and ambiguous stance to avoid being engaged by the patient in a manner characteristic of his other relationships. Such a stance, however, makes it extremely difficult to study through the medium of the patient–therapist relationship, the patient's way of responding to and affecting actual and manifest behaviors of other people. By interpreting and by remaining silent much of the time, the therapist truncates interaction sequences and produces instead expressive monologues.[4]

RESISTANCE TO ACTIVITY: ANALYST REACTION TO ALEXANDER

A hallmark of Freudian psychoanalysis, especially as it has evolved in America, has been an attempt to minimize and restrict the activities of the therapist so as not to interfere with either the unfolding of the transference or the evolution of the patient's autonomy. The therapist trained in a more traditional dynamic format may resist the active stance that examining the here-and-now transference requires. This more active stance may feel new, different, or foreign. We are trained to be silent and to wait rather than go actively after affect in the patient–therapist relationship. Dynamically trained therapists are encouraged to hold their fire until they are sure of the material, and to spend extra time listening, to ensure understanding of the issue in the greatest possible detail.[5] The traditional, dynamic therapist, primarily schooled in the use of quiet listening, evenly suspended attention, and interpretation of free associative material, may feel uncomfortable with a more active engagement. Such attitudes may, however, result in missed opportunity.

Interestingly, some analysts argue that technical recommendation of inactivity differs from Freud's clinical stance, and that modern analysis has emphasized silence and passive listening more than was intended, or is helpful. Racker, in reviewing Freud's work with Dora and the Rat Man, argues that Freud engaged in an active dialogue with the patient.[6] Racker observes that Freud spoke as much as the patient, that he interpreted frequently, and that these interpretations were detailed and extensive. Lipton observes that in the 1940s and 1950s analytic technique became more classic, with therapists becoming more silent and constrained.[3] This technique, according to Lipton, replaced Freud's more personal and interactive approach. The official Freudian position thus became less active and interactive than Freud.

As noted in an earlier chapter, Lipton posits that a prime stimulus in the movement toward a less interactive approach was reaction in the American analytic community to the writings of Franz Alexander, most specifically to his concept of the *corrective emotional experience*.[7] Alexander was interpreted as emphasizing experience at the expense of insight, manipulating rather than analyzing transference, and leaving unresolved the personal attachment which the patient developed toward him. He was understood as using the personal relationship to achieve therapeutic gain at the expense of interpretation. Analyst opposition to Alexander's emphasis on the personal relationship between patient and analyst came to be widely understood as a defense of classical analysis against popular deviation.

Kurt Eissler was among the most vocal in his criticism of what he viewed as Alexander's emphasis on using versus interpreting the patient–therapist relationship. In 1950 Eissler wrote a detailed polemic in which he marshaled arguments against Alexander's position. Soon after, he wrote another paper on technique that continued to expand upon his criticism of Alexander.[8] Here, Eissler presented a basic model for psychoanalytic technique that relied heavily on interpretation and that suggested that any intervention other than interpretation was to be designated as a parameter. This paper was widely read and accepted; the term *parameter* became basic to the vocabulary of analysts. The tenor of this paper was pejorative toward any intervention other than interpretation. Lipton suggests that from this paper a sort of myth arose: the therapist utters no words except interpretation.

From writings such as Eissler's came a tendency to sanction inactivity as correct, and talking as questionable. The use of silence and passive listening gained increased validation as critical aspects of treatment. Indeed, silence is not criticized as systematically as speaking and has gained credence as a technical instrument in psychoanalytically informed methods.[9] A danger is created, however, when silence becomes a technique rather than an indication that the therapist is listening. Listening is not to be confused with silence. Silence for silence's sake is often a result of misunderstanding technique, therapist countertransference, or both. In theory, the therapist is silent so as not to behave in a fashion that unduly influences patient associations. In reality, such a stance often evokes fantasies or activates transferences which require as much interpretation and working through as any other behavior would.

RESISTANCE TO ACTIVITY: THE ENDANGERING OF NEUTRALITY

An active stance has been traditionally seen as endangering therapist neutrality and complicating the development and interpretation of transference. Fenichel, for example, expressed concern that too much activity by the therapist inhibits the patient's trust in the therapist and his willingness to follow the fundamental rule of analysis: open, honest, and spontaneous communication of thoughts and feelings. Through more active engagement, Fenichel saw the therapist as creating the possibility of becoming, in the unconscious of the patient, "a punisher, a repeater of childhood threats, or a magician waving away threats."[10] The therapist's neutrality would be lost and the security of the therapeutic setting, so important for free-flowing communication, would be severely compromised. Accordingly, Fenichel recommended that the therapist strive to create an atmosphere of tolerance which expressed the implicit message: "You will not be punished here, so give your thoughts free rein." In addition to threatening the security of the therapeutic environment, vigorous therapist interventions were thought to distort the natural development of transference. Undue activity by the therapist was thought to muddy the transferential waters, thus making the patient's reactions more difficult to examine and resolve.

Although therapeutic restraint and neutrality seek to provide a secure environment and a clean therapeutic field for transference expression, it must be kept in mind, as Sullivan points out, that one cannot stay outside the field.[11] With his concept of participant observation, Sullivan argues that the therapist is not merely an observer of the patient's mental life but a participant in an interaction with the patient, an interaction that simultaneously influences what one is observing. The therapist can't avoid influencing what he is observing. It is impossible for two people who are together, patient and therapist, not to relate, communicate and influence each other and their interaction. Every action by the therapist, active or passive, will elicit a reaction in the patient. Often it is not easy to know what in the transference are iatrogenic consequences of actual therapist behaviors rather than intrapsychically derived patient behaviors.[12] Specific therapist behaviors elicit specific patient responses. If the therapist criticizes, a certain response is elicited; a different response is elicited to praise, advice, or silence.

The need to establish a safe, facilitative atmosphere in therapy, and to understand the nature of transference reactions, are essential therapeutic tasks. However, inhibiting one's therapeutic involvement (e.g., interpretation, confrontation, clarification) with the patient out of fear of transference distortion does not make identification and work with transference reactions easier. While therapists are often taught to reduce their activity and interaction in order to more clearly highlight transference reactions, it must be kept in mind that lack of activity or nonresponsiveness will elicit a reaction of its own within the patient. Thus, Gill encourages the therapist to keep in mind that the patient responds to what the therapist does *not* do, as well as to what he *does*.[13] The patient reacts to inactivity and unresponsiveness in the therapist; these can become as plausible a basis for an elaboration in the transference as any more active intervention.

> If the analyst remains under the illusion that the current cues he provides to the patient can be reduced to the vanishing point, he may be led into a silent withdrawal, which is not too distant from the caricature of an analyst as someone who does indeed refuse to have any personal relationship with the patient . . . The patient's responses under such conditions can be mistaken for uncontaminated transference when they are in fact transference adaptations to the actuality of the silence.
>
> Merton Gill, 1979, p. 277

NEUTRALITY

Given that the active stance of the therapist, so critical to here-and-now work, may be perceived as affecting the therapist's position of neutrality, it may be helpful to further discuss the concept of neutrality. The neutral stance of the therapist is meant to (1) facilitate, by means of optimal frustration, awareness, and integration of transference longings; (2) protect the therapist from becoming neurotically engaged; and (3) safeguard the patient's autonomy and sense of safety and security within treatment.

OPTIMAL FRUSTRATION: THE EMERGENCE OF TRANSFERENCE

In order for a neurotic to realize the intensity or enormity of his childish desires these desires must be permitted to reach a certain level of insistence. Without this pressure of insistence any interpretive effort is doomed to failure. This is the frustration imposed on patients in analysis or intensive psychotherapy. Without frustration in the therapeutic situation and under the conditions of the therapist gratifying the wishes of the patient, the relationship is closer to an adoption than to therapy. However, some of this adoption may be necessary under certain conditions.

Sidney Tarachow, 1963, p. 274

The neutral stance functions to highlight more clearly the nature of the patient's strivings and the manner in which he attempts to get such strivings met. This allows the patient a more in-depth understanding of himself, of his intrapsychic conflicts and their interpersonal manifestations.

Transference requires a gap between what the patient

wants and what the therapist provides.[14] The stance of neutrality serves to facilitate the emergence of transference by frustrating the patient's wishes for transference gratification. The neutral therapist abstains from responding to the patient's pleas, charges, maneuvers, requests, and demands in the way he would normally respond were this a social relationship. The therapist's failure to gratify the patient's transference wishes results in a sense of frustration for the patient and often increased attempts by the patient to force the therapist to a response that satisfies the patient's neurotic needs. The patient may respond with his customary, albeit neurotic and infantile, means of getting what he wants from the therapist. Menninger refers to this as the patient's conditions for loving and hating.[15]

Frustration of transference acting out highlights the patient's needs and typical methods of relating himself to the significant people in his life to have these needs gratified. With this frustration also comes a heightening in the patient's awareness of the specific wishes that are not being met. Wishes that are not gratified by, and acted out with the therapist move closer to conscious awareness where they can be dealt with on a verbal level. Conflicted childhood longings and all the neurotic interactions which spring from these ambivalent feelings may then be exposed to the conscious adult ego for integration and reorganization at a higher level of development.

Optimal frustration varies from patient to patient. The therapist has the task of monitoring the level of transference frustration that ensues in therapy. Technical skill consists in knowing at what time, in what degree, and in what form the patient's need for response from the analyst should be ministered to in order to maintain the optimal degree of frustration.[15]

Developmental thinking may help clarify the concept of optimal frustration. Children develop under conditions of optimal strain, optimal demand, optimal frustration. Too much strain gets in their way, leading to anxiety, anger, and helplessness at levels that are not constructive; but too little strain, too much gratification, also stands in the way of development.[16] An important function of the mothering object, according to Blanck and Blanck, is "to regulate the frustrations of the critical periods; not to remove frustration, but, when necessary, to impose it, for optimal frustration is structure [and ego] building."[17] Good mothering is viewed as imposing just enough frustration to help the ego develop, but no more. The good-enough mother fails to meet all the child's needs but does so in an optimal manner that provides a situation where the child can manage this failure and develop a bit more in his abilities to perform functions for himself.[18] The good-enough therapist, by providing illumination rather than gratification, containment rather than reenactment, provides similar conditions for the patient.

The problem of optimal frustration is one of the most significant in the therapeutic process. There are significant transference and countertransference motivations to avoid the anxiety resulting from the discovery and maintenance of the "working" level of frustration. Both participants may strive to decrease it.

> No one likes to hurt people — to cause them pain, to stand silently by as they suffer, to withhold help from them when they plead for it. That's where the real wear and tear of analysis lies — in this chronic struggle to keep oneself from doing the things that decent people naturally and spontaneously do. One hears a lot about the abstinence that the analytic patient has to endure, but the abstinence of the analyst is more ruthless and corrosive.
>
> Janet Malcolm, 1981, p. 77

AVOIDANCE OF ENGAGEMENT

The neutral stance of the therapist functions to reduce the degree to which the therapist becomes neurotically engaged with the patient. To maintain the emotional objectivity needed to understand the patient's conflictual and self-defeating interpersonal patterns, the therapist attempts to limit the extent to which he becomes enmeshed in these patterns. The therapist over and over resists the patient's attempt to cast him into a role and relate to him "as if" certain conditions existed.[19] This goal is facilitated by a certain reserve and neutrality. The therapist's self-imposed restraint creates the field in which the patient's illness can manifest itself.[20]

The patient maintains a neurotic interpersonal pattern by provoking behavior in others and by selecting people who have the capacity to play complementary roles in the patient's internalized world of object relations. Wachtel suggests that the patient can't maintain his pattern without accomplices. In the development of a trait there have been many individuals who have served to reinforce the patient's behavior. The pattern is repeated because the patient is able to recreate and evoke similar behavior from new people. "Without the continuing participation of other people, the pattern cannot sustain itself. Therefore it is essential to understand how the patient induces others to act in ways that keep the maladaptive pattern going. It is essential that the patient understand this too."[21]

The therapist may safely assume that whenever a patient experiences recurrent interpersonal conflict, aspects of this conflict will eventually be experienced within the therapeutic relationship. The patient invariably will attempt to elicit from the therapist behavior that is consistent with his internalized views of self and object. The unconscious role relationships between self and object will tend to be actualized in his current interpersonal relations.[20] The patient may seek to draw from the therapist behaviors consonant with the role assigned to the object in the patient's scenario, or conversely the role assigned to the self. In the latter case the patient will tend toward a personal reenactment of the object representation.[22] A patient, for example, may recreate the scenario of guilty child and punitive parent, this scenario being very common in his upbringing. Depending on the situation, the patient may reenact the role of the guilty child or punitive parent. The therapist, pressured by means of projective identification, will be provoked to enact the complementary role. In projective identification the patient projects (externalizes) an aspect of the self (either a self or object representation) onto another person and then attempts to induce the person to behave in a fashion congruent with the projection.[23]

The possibility of role reversal in the patient's externalization of his internalized object world has gained increasing attention and does much to aid in understanding the patient's interpersonal relations. A more traditional view had the patient reenacting a role assigned to a self representation, with the therapist being coerced to play the complementary role assigned to the object.

The patient's behavior tends to evoke a restricted aspect of the therapist's own internal experience and behavioral repertoire. The therapist cannot avoid being hooked or neurotically engaged by the patient.[24] The patient is more adept and more expert in his distinctive pattern of interpersonal encounter. The patient pulls complementary responses through his overpracticed, rehearsed, and rigid means of relating. He has had years of practice and skill to engage others; his psychological survival may seem, to the patient, to depend on it.

The therapist thus will be led to behave in ways that

validate the patient's view of himself, others, and the world in general. While he cannot avoid being drawn into a reciprocal role, the question is whether he can recognize what is happening and work his way out of it.[25] It is not an error for the therapist to become engaged; it is, however, to remain so. The neutral stance of the therapist is of value in that it allows him to restrict his enactment of complementary roles. The therapist allows a partial engagement in order to understand the interactive patterns of the patient from the inside; he tastes, but does not swallow whole. This allows him not only to participate in the patient's internalized object world but also to draw back, to work his way out, in order to shed light on its structure. Adherence to the concept of neutrality, to objectivity and emotional restraint, allows the therapist to regress in service of the ego in order to experience, but then to return to adult, secondary-process functioning to make sense of it.

The therapeutic effort is to try to get a grasp of the manner in which the patient recreates his problem with you in the transference. . . . You stay with the patient until you become important to him, and when you are important you play out some role that has been assigned you.

Sidney Tarachow, 1963, p. 253

ENHANCEMENT OF PATIENT SAFETY AND AUTONOMY

The more plainly the analyst lets it be seen that he is proof against every temptation, the more readily he will be able to extract from the situation its analytic content.

Sigmund Freud, 1915, p. 160

The therapist's stance of neutrality provides a structure which promotes an opening-up by the patient, a type of communication that is neither appropriate nor sanctioned in other interpersonal contexts.[26] On one hand, the neutrality of the therapist becomes a source of frustration for the patient, in that the feelings become increasingly manifest and conscious, but are not responded to in a manner that the patient is accustomed to or wishes. At the same time, however, the therapist's neutral stance is a source of reassurance, in that it permits the patient an opportunity to express thoughts and feelings previously defended against, without having to take immediate responsibility for them, or to be afraid that they will lead to some type of response, reciprocal or otherwise. The therapist's neutrality, his attempt to maintain objectivity, to avoid unduly influencing or controlling the patient, as well as to avoid being unduly influenced or controlled, contributes to the patient's sense of safety and autonomy within the therapy. This provides conditions for a more spontaneous and deeper expression of feelings, thereby facilitating the patient's awareness and expression of transference material.

Neutrality furthers the patient's willingness to expose aspects of himself which are normally denied, repressed, or warded off. Strachey teaches that the neutrality and nonjudgmentalness of the therapist are critical in that the patient initially hands his superego over to the therapist. "The patient in analysis tends to accept the analyst in some way or other as a substitute for his own superego."[27] As a reaction to this, the patient then becomes very sensitive to what he perceives to be the therapist's reaction to and perceptions of him. If the therapist becomes critical of patient attitudes and impulses, the patient may become resistant to communicating them, thus losing the opportunity for exploration and understanding.

It is important to note that whether the therapist becomes

an adversary or an ally of the patient's position, it becomes increasingly difficult for the patient to explore and examine it. Becoming the patient's adversary impedes communication in what may seem, to the patient, a hostile environment, whereas supporting the patient's position often reinforces externalizing defenses and an ensuing persecutory orientation.[28] In addition, taking the patient's side may lead the patient to fear a future loss of therapist support. He may thus become hesitant in revealing anything that may affect the therapist's positive view of him.

The concept of neutrality also must be kept in mind when the therapist is tempted to express judgments regarding significant others in the patient's life. Though a patient may present a parent or spouse in an unfavorable light, he is often consciously identified with this person. Judgment of the spouse, for instance, may become judgement of the patient. The parent who is consciously hated may be unconsciously loved and admired. Finally, making a judgment toward another may communicate that the patient is also being judged, though silently and often unconsciously.

A caveat in regard to use of a neutral stance to promote safety and free communication: The therapist may use a silent, restrained, neutral stance as a rationalization for his affective isolation and schizoid tendencies. The here-and-now interchange, including the examination and description of the patient's interpersonal process, may be avoided not so much to maintain neutrality but because it stirs up therapist discomfort. While providing little or no feedback to the patient regarding interpersonal impact is often done under the auspices of maintaining the beneficial effects of neutrality, this lack of feedback can have another effect. The therapist's stance can often increase patient anxiety leading him to feel less safe. Without feedback and interchange, the patient may sense disapproval with everything he says. In such a situation, one's proclivities for experiencing disapproval are given free rein, creating anxiety that may be responded to with increasing defensiveness, as opposed to openness.[29] This lack of feedback thrusts the patient back upon his own fantasies. This may be productive if it can be used to correct misperception, but such fantasies often damage the therapeutic alliance and lead to an iatrogenic reaction to the treatment in which reality and transference cannot be distinguished. "So long as the analyst hides behind a 'neutral' self-presentation, so long as his own participation in the session's events does not become part of the focus of what he discusses with the patient, it remains difficult for the patient to understand his own experience, and how he goes about creating and recreating it in his daily life."[30]

NEUTRALITY: OPTIMAL STANCE

The patient was silent and then he laughed. . . . I asked what he thought the laugh meant. He said he was pleased by my attitude. "You leave everything as it is. You illuminate. You do not try to control or change anything."

Theodore Dorpat, 1977, p. 53

The therapist's attitude of neutrality assists the patient in finding himself, in following his own blueprint, without living up to the therapist's ideals.[31] It means taking nothing for granted without being cynical, and being able to tolerate ambiguity, incomplete closure, and alternate views.[32] During this process, in which the therapist both observes and participates, neutrality reflects the ability to stay curious, open, and empathic regardless of those situations in which the patient strives to elicit some thing else. Neutrality does not imply emotional unavailability to the patient. It does not preclude an empathic, authentic, warm attitude on the part of the therapist, but, to the contrary, may best reflect such warmth and empathy under conditions in which the emergence of the patient's aggression in the transference would naturally bring about counteraggressive reactions in the therapist.[33]

Neutrality is constantly threatened and interfered with; a good part of the therapist's efforts will have to be devoted to reestablishing it, again and again. Due to the complex interplay between therapist and patient, the optimal stance of therapeutic neutrality is never fully realized—or not for long, if it is. Schafer argues, however, that to recognize human limitation and variability is not to conclude that it is useless or foolish to attempt to set forth standards of excellence for one's work. "For it is on the individual analyst's efforts to approximate this ideal that the beneficial effects of analyzing largely depend."[34]

COMPLICATIONS OF ACTIVITY

> The listening process becomes more complex as the analyst feels freer to use himself interactively.
>
> Philip Bromberg, 1984, p. 33

Considerations of neutrality do not preclude the therapist taking an active stance vis-à-vis the patient's transference reactions. The therapist can actively confront, explore, and interpret patient material without compromising his neutrality. Taking such an active stance is critical in here-and-now work as the therapist persistently questions, points out, describes, and provides feedback as to what seems to be occurring between patient and therapist. This may be done under the umbrella of a neutral, nonjudgmental, and nondirective stance.

Greater activity and risk-taking by the therapist may potentially entail certain complications for the treatment which may need therapeutic attention.[35] These include the following:

1. The increased activity level of the therapist may suggest to the patient that the therapist does a majority of the work in therapy, thus conveying a distorted sense of responsibility. The patient may inadvertently be encouraged to become a spectator of his own treatment, where the patient provides information while the therapist-as-expert provides solutions for the patient's difficulties.

2. The aggressive components inherent in the therapist's increased activity level may threaten the patient and induce an identification with the aggressor in which the patient works compliantly, but superficially, with the therapist. The patient needs some sense of safety with the therapist before softening his defenses and more honestly expressing thoughts and feelings. An attacking, exhorting stance may create more passive submission than authentic expression of important concerns.

3. The patient may become overstimulated by the therapist and spend unproductive energy trying to make sense of the therapist's behavior.

4. Preoccupation with early and active interpretation of resistance and transference manifestations may result in the therapist's becoming more concerned with formulating interventions than with listening. In such situations, the patient may feel emotionally unconnected with the therapist.

5. In the process of learning to respond more spontaneously, the therapist has an increased likelihood of being wrong in a formulation or misunderstood while offering an interpretation. The therapist may feel burned, guilty, or defeated

when his efforts do not have their intended effect. He may then lose confidence in the treatment format.

6. The more active, interactive nature of here-and-now work may result in greater susceptibility to having the patient's adaptive defenses undermined and to the therapist becoming involved in neurotic acting out.

Chapter Eight

Overemphasis of Positive Transference

At no time from his first psychoanalytic writings to his last did Freud ever lose sight of or minimize the importance of the affective relationship between patient and analyst. Throughout his work on the process of treatment a kind of running battle may be detected between the respective claims of understanding and attachment, although when one looks more closely one sees that it is not equal combat, but a struggle for survival on the part of understanding. To be sure, Freud was very much the champion of the voice of reason, but while he was cheering it on, he seemed to be advising his friends not to bet on it.

Lawrence Friedman, 1978 p. 526

Therapists may obstruct here-and-now work by an overreliance on the development and maintenance of a warm, supportive positive transference relationship. Uses and misuses of positive transference will be addressed in this chapter.

THE UNOBJECTIONABLE POSITIVE TRANSFERENCE

> *It remains the first aim of the treatment to attach him to it and to the person of the doctor. To ensure this, nothing need be done but to give him time. If one exhibits a serious interest in him, carefully clears away the resistances that crop up at the beginning and avoids making certain mistakes, he will of himself form such an attachment and link the doctor up with one of the images of the people by whom he was accustomed to be treated with affection.*
>
> Sigmund Freud, 1913, p. 139

Freud felt that a strong relationship between patient and therapist was critical, and was indeed the vehicle of success in treatment. He termed this friendly, affectionate, reality-oriented attachment of patient to therapist the *unobjectionable positive transference*. This portion of the patient's transference reaction was seen by Freud as having "passed through the full process of psychical development," "is directed towards reality," and "at the disposal" of the conscious personality.[1] The unobjectionable positive transference was viewed as facilitating rapport between patient and therapist. It was differentiated from two other components of transference: the transference of negative, hostile impulses and the transference of repressed erotic impulses. The hostile and erotic transferences were seen as obstructions to the treatment process and were the objects of analysis, whereas the unobjectionable positive transference was fostered and viewed as the bond which allows analysis to proceed.

The unobjectionable positive transference today goes by a number of other names — *basic transference, mature transference* — or else is subsumed under more comprehensive concepts such as the *therapeutic* or *working alliance*.[2] While the exact meaning of these terms may vary, they all reflect the importance dynamic therapists place in the development of a strong, trusting patient-therapist relationship. For purposes of the present discussion, this relationship will be referred to as positive transference. It is viewed as representing both the patient's response to the reality of the treatment setting, that is, to the actual interactions that occur, and as a displacement of the patient's childhood wishes to trust and to be treated affectionately by parental figures.

USE OF POSITIVE TRANSFERENCE

How do you motivate people to get back into the world? By letting them fall in love with you. How else?

Elvin Semrad, 1980, p. 120

Although a basic ingredient of psychotherapy is the healing quality of the patient–therapist relationship, there is no consensus as to how this occurs or exactly how the relationship is to be used. Within the analytic literature there exists an uneasy coexistence of two conflicting views regarding the therapeutic relationship.[3] One stresses the importance of neutrality and the use of interpretation to facilitate insight, understanding, and growth. The other view is epitomized by the emotionally involved and responsive therapist who exercises therapeutic influence through all aspects of an affectively intense patient–therapist relationship. This may include, yet go beyond, the verbal interpretive mode in order to support and actualize. In this approach, empathy, attachment, and gratification of specific, selected needs is favored.

Sidestepping, for the present, the controversy surrounding the efficacy of the neutral/interpretive versus the empathic/reconstructive approaches, it is likely that most dynamic therapists would agree that an important function of the positive transference comes in its use as a motivating force for the patient to tolerate the anxieties and frustration inherent to the therapeutic process. Indeed, Freud felt that positive transference provided the basic motivation for the patient's continued work in the therapy: "[It] is the strongest motive of the analysand for cooperating in the work of analysis."[4] The wish of the patient to obtain or maintain the good will of the therapist is of major importance in overcoming the patient's resistance to self-exploration and change. The positive transference has a critical role in the utilization of interpretations: "It is what enables the patient to listen to them and take them seriously!"[5] This warm, trusting attachment, this wish to please and be pleasing to the therapist, helps the patient cope with the stress and discomfort that occur during the therapeutic investigation. The patient's trust, confidence, and warm feelings for the therapist often allow the patient to endure temporary anxiety and confusion, and to continue the psychotherapy process.[6] To the extent the patient develops a positive transference, he is able to keep alive the potential for a good object-relationship through the inevitable stages of resistance.[7]

The importance of a strong therapeutic attachment may be conceptualized in a different manner. The therapeutic alliance has the function of keeping regression in therapy on a productive level.[8] With a constructive regression, infantile conflict is reopened to be reworked and reorganized to increase mastery. As the patient's defenses are gently undermined, unconscious drives focus increasingly on the therapist. A strong alliance is needed to cope with this. When the patient regresses he must be allied enough with the therapist to be able to deal with the emerging feelings. It is likely that only with a sound alliance will the patient risk the uncovering of unconscious conflict.

> *We require the patient to abandon his infantile objects, and offer adult objects in exchange. Without this incentive perhaps no treatment of any kind would be possible.*
>
> Sidney Tarachow, 1963, p. 21

OVEREMPHASIS OF POSITIVE TRANSFERENCE

Here-and-now work requires a willingness for honest interchange around therapist–patient interaction. The therapist examines, and encourages the patient to examine the nature of their interaction and of the patient's relationship predispositions. The patient's defensive patterns will often be confronted. This may stir up anxiety and hostility but must be done in order to take a look at the actual underpinnings of the patient's relationship patterns. The therapist may resist here-and-now work by an undue focus on developing a strong positive helping image vis-à-vis the patient. The therapist may emphasize maintaining, at all costs, an overly supportive, comfortable, and low-tension relationship which accentuates the gratifying, and avoids the frustrating, aspects of therapy. This will make it difficult for patient and therapist to examine their relationship most productively.

PROBLEMS WITH OVEREMPHASIS OF POSITIVE TRANSFERENCE

The therapist's stance vis-à-vis the patient will have a great effect on what type of reaction is evoked in the patient. The therapist who gratifies his patient will most often elicit an attitude of gratitude by the patient (at least consciously). Such behavior interferes with subsequent transference development, particularly the transference of hostile, angry feelings. The patient may find it difficult to become angry with a therapist who has provided him immeasurable support and gratification. Becoming an overly kind, gratifying object impedes the patient's ability to project his bad introjects onto the therapist, making it difficult to identify and explore them. The patient's conflicts with aggression thus can't be worked on.

The therapist who is always kind and obliging, and who avoids confrontation, will reinforce the repression of the patient's responses to being frustrated. He will never view the patient's aggression, his typical means of managing disappointment and anger, and will never have the *in vivo* opportunity to examine and treat the conflict imbedded in these responses. Inhibition of patient aggression may lead to an acting out of these feelings outside of treatment. It may also result in an overly dependent transference relationship which simultaneously expresses the patient's hostility through the sticky, clinging nature of the relationship while defending against such feeling by means of the positive feelings that the patient consciously has for the therapist.[9]

An additional complication regarding the inhibition of patient aggression is the important role expression of anger and aggression plays in the emotional development of the patient/child. Anger is part of a developmentally appropriate thrust toward separation from the therapist/mother.[10] Suppression of the patient's aggression may inhibit the gradual attainment of psychological separation.

A warm, supportive atmosphere within therapy is valued because internalization of the therapist as a helpful, supportive, and affirming figure is more likely to occur in a positive affective climate.[9] Although the beneficial effects of such internalization are evident, the therapist is encouraged to heed the caution of Heimann regarding the therapist falling into an idealized, "all-good" role vis-à-vis the patient.[11] Heimann observed that patients long to escape the pressure of their own cruel introjects, now residing in their superego, by introjecting the idealized image of a kind, benign therapist. While the superego may be modified somewhat through contact with a benign therapist, substantive change in the superego results from working through of one's impulses, anxieties, and conflict. Unless this is done the patient will engage in an unconscious oscillation between the idealization of the kind therapist and the persecutory feelings related to his image of his original parents; the patient's superego becomes a savior or a demon, overly indulgent or excessively punitive.

An additional caveat concerning the use of a positive transference to encourage identification with the internalization of the therapist: idealization of the therapist often leads to the establishment of a tenacious transference bondage which is analogous to the attachment often fostered by organized religions. This attachment may bring about a massive, versus realistic and aim-inhibited, identification with the therapist and thus hamper attainment of the patient's own identity.[12]

> *The adult patient possesses distorted internalizations, but is not an empty vessel into which benign experiences can be poured.*
>
> Rubin and Gertrude Blanck, 1977, p. 39

COUNTERTRANSFERENCE IMPLICATIONS

Therapists' undue emphasis on the maxim "the relationship cures," may be related to the anxieties inherent in here-and-now examination of the transference relationship. These anxieties often relate to unresolved countertransference issues. The therapeutic interaction often stirs up therapist anxieties regarding loveableness, self-worth, loneliness, and the need of emotional contact. Such feelings may lead a cultivation of positive transference. The need to feel important and be in control, and the inability to maintain self-esteem independently of the idealization of others may also heighten this tendency.

The therapist may overemphasize positive transference due to personal conflict with aggressive impulses. Difficulties in tolerating the patient's anger as well as one's own aggressive wishes often leads to defenses of a reaction-formation nature. The result is often a therapist who comes across as an overly benevolent, reparative figure.[13] Such therapists may lean toward placating behavior and often find it too difficult to set firm limits when necessary. As Winnicott observes, if one is unable to admit to hate, one often falls back upon masochism.[14]

Another countertransference-based resistance to here-and-now transference analysis is alluded to by Bird when he discusses what help and relief the therapist can provide by enabling the patient to tell his life story, confess his guilt, express his ambitions, and explore his confusions. The learning-about-life resulting from the therapist's skilled questions, observations, and interpretations offers further help. Taken altogether, the total *real* value to the patient of the therapeutic situation can easily be immense. The trouble with this kind of help, according to Bird, is that, "if it goes on and on, it may have such a real, direct, and continuing impact upon the patient that he can never get deeply enough involved in transference situations to allow him to resolve or even to become acquainted with his most crippling internal difficulties."[15] Direct helpfulness is very seductive for *both* patient and therapist. It may, and often does, lead the therapist to develop and maintain the role of a wise, benevolent helper with little work being done with the patient's here-and-now transference manifestations. This failure to adequately develop and work with transference is one of the major reasons a psychodynamic treatment may fail.

Chapter Nine

Difficulties in Differentiating Transference from Nontransference

Not everything is transference that is experienced by a patient in the form of affects and impulses during the course of an analytic treatment. If the analysis appears to make no progress, the patient has . . . the right to be angry, and his anger need not be a transference from childhood—or rather we will not succeed in demonstrating the transference component in it. . . .

Otto Fenichel, 1941, p. 95

Here-and-now transference analysis may be compromised by the therapist's inability to work with the patient on differentiating transference from nontransference behavior. Difficulties in differentiation are viewed as relating to: (1) therapist resistance to the actual process of sorting out realistic from transference-based reactions and (2) perplexities inherent in distinguishing transference from reality.

THERAPIST RESISTANCE

The therapist may obstruct here-and-now transference analysis by failing to differentiate between transference and nontransference phenomena. Suppose the therapist is a few minutes late for an appointment and his patient expresses feelings about this. Effective work with transference would suggest that therapist and patient sort out what feelings are the result of the therapist's being late and what may be a resurrection of narcissistic injury from the past. This sifting through of what is a realistic reaction and what is a displaced reaction is a potentially vexing task demanding much of both patient and therapist. The difficulties associated with this process often result in its avoidance. Continuing with the above example, the therapist could intervene by treating the patient's reaction to his lateness as totally appropriate and justified by his behavior. He could offer a brief apology to mollify the patient and hope to get on with other issues. Such an intervention, while often accepted by the patient, may convey to him a reluctance to explore his feelings and discomfort with interchange regarding their here-and-now relationship.

Alternatively, the therapist could treat the patient's reaction to his lateness as totally transference based. A major problem with analytic work is the therapist's tendency to attribute the patient's reaction entirely to the patient's internal processes, with the therapist frequently failing to look at how the therapist may have actually created, or at least contributed to, the reaction.[1] Such a stance undermines the therapeutic alliance and limits the patient's ability to make use of the therapist's observations. Defensive behavior may be elicited as the patient becomes angry with the therapist's unwillingness to own up to consequences of his behavior; further exploration is resisted.

Therapists too often include all attitudes that a patient has toward the therapist as transference. Such a stance toward patient perceptions may be used defensively. Szasz comments that patient reactions do not come prelabeled and that the labeling of a reaction as transference is a judgment formed by the therapist.[2] Citing the concept of transference as Freud's greatest single contribution, Szasz posits that it may serve two separate purposes: (1) it is a crucial part of the patient's therapeutic experience, and (2) it is a successful defensive measure which protects the therapist from overly intense affective and real-life involvement with the patient. In discovering the concept of transference, Freud was able to step back from the affective intensities of the patient–therapist relationship that were the undoing of Breuer. If the patient loves or hates the therapist, and if the therapist can view these attitudes as transference, the therapist has, in effect, convinced himself that the patient does not have these feelings or disposition toward him. "The patient does not really love or hate the analyst, but someone else. What could be more convincing?"[3]

While this use of transference is enormously facilitating, and a stroke of genius, in that it buffers both parties from the immediate impact of potentially powerful feelings while one tries to make sense of them, Szasz argues that transference provides a ready-made opportunity for putting the patient at arm's length. It supports a distancing of the therapist from the interaction, that is, "he's not reacting to me but to what I represent." Although helpful in that it supplies the therapist with the emotional space and detachment which may be needed to intervene therapeutically, care must be taken to avoid interpreting behavior that makes the therapist anxious as transference in order to escape its emotional impact and its possible implications concerning the therapist's behavior.

Failure to differentiate transference from nontransference by rigidly viewing all patient reactions as realistic responses to the therapist, or rote assignment of all patient reactions to the transference realm may be a resistance to the affect involved in the here-and-now experience and a defense against the impact of the patient–therapist relationship. The therapist's ability to conduct a balanced exploration regarding what is realistic and what is transference based requires openness, flexibility, and tolerance of uncertainty/ambiguity. It is often much easier to retreat to the relative shelter of an either-or approach to avoid the anxiety inherent in the sorting through. In such cases an opportunity for collaboration, alliance, and further insight is lost.

Designating transference as not-real in the analytic situation afforded the analyst the protected role of detached observer vis-à-vis the intensities on both sides of the couch.

James McLaughlin, 1981, p. 659

INHERENT PERPLEXITIES IN DISTINGUISHING TRANSFERENCE FROM REALITY

The patient–therapist relationship does not readily lend itself to an effective sorting out of transference from nontransference phenomena. The following are seen as contributing to this: (1) transference and reality are interdependent concepts, (2) reality is constructed as much as perceived, and (3) the therapist both participates in and observes the interaction he is attempting to understand.

THE INTERDEPENDENCE OF TRANSFERENCE AND REALITY

A conservative view of the therapeutic relationship posits a dichotomy between transference and nontransference.[4] This view holds that the patient (in part), and the therapist (primarily), are able to determine the difference between transference and realistic perception. It has been argued, however, that the dichotomy drawn between transference as distortion and nontransference as realistic does violence to the actual nature of the relationship between patient and therapist.[5] Transference and reality are interdependent concepts which rely on each other for their existence. Just as there is no reality without transference, there is no transference without reality. Loewald observes that it would be erroneous to imply that the realistic relationship has nothing to do with transference. "There is neither such a thing as reality nor a real relationship, without transference. Any real relationship involves the transfer of unconscious images to present day objects."[6] McLaughlin similarly asserts that all we feel we know or can ever come to know about ourselves and the world, our psychic reality, can be ours only through psychic structuring shaped by transference.[7]

The patient's perception of the therapist is an amalgam of feelings and attitudes representing childhood predisposition (transference) and adult ego-functioning (reality). There is a mutual coloration and blending between these two with the relative influence of each in a constant state of flux and movement. While the degree to which a patient's experience of here-and-now relationship is influenced by past or present may vary widely across patients, and may change markedly from point to point in the therapy, the idea of an attitude determined solely either by the past or by the present is an abstraction. According to Gill, "no matter how inappropriate behavior is, it has some relation to the present, and no matter how appropriate it is, it has some relation to the past."[8]

REALITY IS CONSTRUCTED AS WELL AS PERCEIVED

Reality is not a preestablished given or absolute. The individual plays an active role in the shaping and defining of his experience of self and others. Wachtel, in citing the work of Piaget on cognitive development, asserts that individuals do not respond directly to stimuli per se, but are constructing reality every bit as much as perceiving it. We are not stimuli-bound and do not reflexively respond to external stimuli, but rather selectively organize and make sense of new input in terms of the experiences and structures that define who we are. In this context, transference may be understood as the tendency to experience events in terms of structures and expectations based on earlier experiences.[9] It is a means of constructing as well as construing a relationship.

THE THERAPIST PARTICIPATES AND OBSERVES

The therapist has an inescapable involvement in all that goes on in the interview; and to the extent that he is unconscious or unwitting of his participation in the interview, to that extent he does not know what is happening.

H. S. Sullivan, Unpublished Manuscript

Differentiation of transference from nontransference phenomena is further complicated by the fact that the therapist influences and is influenced by the very situation he is attempting to understand. It is not always easy to ascertain what in a patient's perception is the result of his personal psychology, and what is a realistic response to the therapist's behavior. The essence of Sullivan's concept of participant observation is that the observer is always influencing what he observes. The patient's reaction to the therapist is influenced by his perception of the therapist, whose behavior is, in turn, influenced by the patient. A certain interlocking of transference and countertransference occurs.[10] Each reciprocally affects the other. Only by means of a rigid belief in the therapist as blank screen could the therapist conceive the patient's responses as emanating entirely from within the patient.[11]

Realization that the response of the therapist will influence subsequent responses by the patient has often led therapists to become overly constrictive, inhibited, and rigid vis-à-vis their relationship with the patient. Noting that this may be carried to an unhelpful extreme, Gill suggests that the therapist worry less about influencing and more about exploring the patient's experience regarding the therapist.[11]

While the therapist cannot neutralize his personality or behavior, he needs to take into account how he influences the patient's experience of him. In ascertaining the patient's experience of the relationship, the therapist must be alert not only for the attitudes the patient has but also the attitudes the patient believes the therapist has toward the patient.[11] Exploration of perceived attitudes in the therapist often facilitates the patient's discussion of his own feelings toward the therapist.

> *No matter that the therapist saw himself as pure observer, he always was a participant in a relationship, for better or worse.*
>
> Edwin Kasin, 1977, p. 365

TRANSFERENCE RESIDUE: THE THERAPIST'S CONTRIBUTION TO TRANSFERENCE

It has been increasingly recognized that the actual behaviors and attributes of the therapist play a role in evoking transference reactions. Transference distortions often have a reality hook or peg on which they are hung.[12] This current stimulus for the transference is referred to by Gill as a *transference residue* in analogy to the *dream day residue*.[13] While the range of events which may stimulate transference reaction is wide, the therapist is encouraged to be mindful that the patient's reactions are never completely unrelated to what transpires within the therapy.

Transference residue may be difficult to identify in that the patient may be responding to something in the therapist's behavior that may seem trivial to the therapist (e.g, a fleeting offhand comment). Fenichel observes that "one is again and again surprised by the relative insignificance of the actual occurrences during analysis that serve as occasions for transference reactions."[14] The patient's response may seem to be something that appears trivial to the patient as well as the therapist. As in displacement to a trivial aspect of the day residue of a dream, displacement can better serve resistance when it is to something trivial.

Because it is connected to conflict-laden material, the stimulus to the transference may be difficult to find. It may quickly be disavowed, with its presence in the patient's awareness being only transitory. This disavowal may be a repeat of a disavowal in earlier life, in that the patient may have learned, for defensive purposes, to disavow the connection between a person's behavior and the reaction to this behavior (and person).[15] The ability to identify how and when this disavowal occurs can be of great benefit.

DOES THE STIMULUS JUSTIFY THE RESPONSE?

Here-and-now work strives to more clearly understand the patient's experience of the therapeutic relationship, and to learn what in the therapist's behavior is being used by the patient to justify his reactions. The transference response always has a plausible basis in the here and now. Interpretation of transference begins with relating it to something presently happening in therapy. The patient's perception of the therapist as being controlling, for instance, is best managed by avoiding a genetic interpretation and investigating what has occurred in the here and now that seems to the patient to justify his feelings. It is helpful for the therapist to continually seek to understand what it is about his behavior that may have made the patient's experience of him possible.

By examining what the therapist has done to create the patient's reaction, or how he has contributed to it, the stage is set for the patient to explore his means of viewing people and interactions. Therapist and patient strive to understand what the patient is responding to and whether this stimulus justifies the patient's experience. If the transference residue is ascertained as not being sufficient to cause the response, possible transferential components to this reaction may then be explored. This sequence of establishing what the patient is responding to and then mutually deciding whether the stimulus justifies the response, does much to enlist the patient's willingness to explore his personal contribution to his reaction. Thus Gill writes: "If an examination of the basis for the [patient's] conclusion makes clear that the actual situation . . . is subject to other meanings than the one the patient has reached, he will more readily consider his pre-existing bias, that is his transference."[16]

The ability to ascertain the reality peg for transference reactions enables the patient to begin examination of the manner in which situations are perceived and interpreted; of how preconceived notions, expectations, and bias may influence perceptions, and how these perceptual sets may create problems. Such work also helps identify situations where the patient's perceptions are *not* problematic and for developing an appreciation of the patient's strengths.[17] The patient may learn what situations are handled with little difficulty. The importance of focusing on identifying patient strengths, though often relegated to treatment of an ego-supportive nature, is a critical component of all treatment.

FLEXIBILITY VS. RIGIDITY

Transference resistance is . . . to be worked through primarily because of the rigidity it imposes on the patient, not because of the important secret that it conceals.

Arnold Cooper, 1987, pp. 81–82

A goal of here-and-now work is the development of a consensually validated understanding of the nature of the patient–therapist relationship. The development of such an understanding is often difficult. It must be kept in mind that there are only ways of approximating reality, there is no context-free reality to use as a criterion for examining the relationship.[18] The therapist may find it helpful to focus on the rigidity versus flexibility of the patient's interpersonal attitude rather than on what is realistic versus what is distorted.[5] The patient's distorting tendencies are deemphasized. Instead comes a focus on the number of ways to view a situation plausibly and how the patient chooses to accept a particular one. The patient is helped to consider that the situation is subject to more interpretations than the one he has reached. Subsequently he is encouraged to investigate how his interpretation of events may in part be derived by what he has brought to the relationship. It may be less important to "correct" distortions of reality as it is to help the patient understand his investment in rigidly and selectively perceiving and constructing events.[11] To illustrate:

A patient who had experienced the emotional withdrawal from mother in response to displeasing behavior perceived the therapist's quiet listening at the onset of the session as punitive and withholding. This led to anger and its passive-aggressive expression (i.e., the patient became silent and withheld his thoughts and feelings). A therapeutic impasse resulted. The patient's expectations of the therapist and his perceptions of the therapist's behavior were discussed. The therapist explained how he perceived the situation and what he was attempting to do by his quiet listening (i.e., to give the patient the opportunity to decide what to discuss, to allow room for the patient to freely explore feelings). This discussion allowed the patient to consider the possibility that the therapist's motives behind his behavior were perhaps dissimilar to that of his mother. The patient was able to step back from his behavior and consider alternative views as to what may be going on between him and his therapist. While still sensitive to silence, the patient was able to collaborate more readily. The therapist, in turn, was alerted to the patient's difficulty in trusting the ultimate benevolence of the therapist's intention. He was then able to offer empathic acknowledgment of the struggle between self-expression and withdrawal. Such work strengthened the therapeutic alliance and offered the patient a corrective experience around conflict resolution.

Helping the patient consider that his perceptions and reactions to the therapist are subject to conclusions and interpretations other than what he has come up with is not an attempt to convince the patient that his perceptions are inaccurate, but rather to help him become more flexible in the manner in which situations are reacted to.

Chapter Ten

Posture of Certainty

The analyst cannot be certain he's right, nor can he prove it.

Merton Gill, 1982, p. 118

The therapist may resist examination of here-and-now transference material by assuming a posture of certainty regarding the accuracy of his ideas concerning the relationship and the patient. This posture of certainty may represent a retreat from an examination of feelings and perceptions and may compromise development of an ongoing sense of investigative collaboration needed for the patient to benefit from treatment.

COMPLICATIONS WITH A POSTURE OF CERTAINTY

Nothing is more harmful to the analysis than a school-masterish, or even an authoritative, attitude on the physician's part. Anything we say to the patient should be put to him in the form of a tentative suggestion and not of a confidently held opinion, not only to avoid irritating him, but because there is always the possibility that we may be mistaken. It is an old commercial custom to put "E & OE" ("errors and omissions excepted") at the bottom of every calculation, and every analytic statement should be put forward with the same qualification.
Sandor Ferenczi, 1928, p. 94

It is not unreasonable to assume that the therapist's view of the therapeutic encounter is more objective, unbiased, and less distorted than that of the patient. Freud, for instance, argues that in discrepancies between patient and therapist on observations or memories, the therapist observation is more likely to be correct due to the fact that the therapist is less likely to be emotionally involved.[1] Schafer similarly emphasizes that the therapist's greater expertise, distance from the conflict, and different responsibilities within the session, place the therapist in a more objective position.[2] Cooper furthermore suggests the patient, in the neurotic areas of his psychic functioning, has to some degree unconsciously constricted and distorted his perceptual, affective, and cognitive capacities.[3]

While it is reasonable to presume the therapist's view to be more objective, one never knows for certain. And while it is important for the therapist to communicate trust and confidence in his observations, a posture of certainty concerning his opinion complicates effective here-and-now work. The playing of an omnipotent role by the therapist creates a one-up situation which compromises the investigative collaboration one hopes to develop within the therapy. A brilliant, deep, or far-reaching interpretation, delivered by an overbearing therapist, is assimilated quite differently than an understanding that is the joint product of an ongoing patient–therapist collaboration. The omnipotent, all-knowing therapist colludes with the demoralized patient's wish for nurturance from a superior being (i.e., parental figure).[4] This has a variety of effects, many of them detrimental. For example, while therapist assumption of the role of prophet, savior, and redeemer may facilitate conflict solution by means of gross identification, such a stance also impedes the patient's integration of his own psychological structures and of the gradual building up of new ones.[5]

The more the therapist plays guru, the more the patient is

reinforced to present a weak, empty, fragmented ego to the therapist in hopes of receiving his ministrations.[2] The therapist who is all-knowledgeable, in total control and certain of all observations, encourages the patient to assume the role of a weak, unsure, ineffectual individual vis-à-vis the therapist in hopes of being supported and cared for, much as the parent provides for the dependent child. It is infantilizing to tell the patient what is true and to assume responsibility for the patient in figuring out his life; it is also seductive, particularly with those patients possessing strong underlying urges to regress to a passive-receptive and dependent position to avoid the anxieties inherent in present-day autonomous functioning.

In cautioning the therapist to resist the temptation to make clever interpretations, Strupp and Binder argue that attempts to provide definitive observations may foreclose further inquiry and are not as helpful as the interpretive pointing to topics possibly worth examining. The latter is viewed as fostering a process of mutual curiosity and exploration. "The best interpretations are the ones the patient gradually learns to make."[6] The therapist thus can be too quick to provide answers and solutions and to arbitrate reality for the patient. Assumption of a parental role encourages passivity and a reticence in exercising critical ego functions. This subverts the therapeutic task of teaching that one accomplishes to the degree one puts forth effort. Self-reliance and confidence in one's own abilities are compromised.

Greenacre highlights a related difficulty in the therapist becoming the arbitrator of the patient's reality.[7] She cautions the therapist to avoid the position where the therapist must analyze reality for the patient (i.e., where the therapist becomes responsible for nailing down the objective situation for the patient). Such a stance will pull the therapist toward analyzing the patient's whole life situation and the people in it, and less toward analyzing the patient and his attitudes to various aspects of his life. The result may be that the patient imitates the therapist and begins to focus on analyzing motives of others, with less focus on his own motives. The therapist, according to Greenacre, has the task of facilitating or guiding the patient to his own interpretation of the situation and less to giving an interpretation.

Therapist tendency toward omniscience and omnipotence may initially be accepted, perhaps relished, but later will stir up therapeutic resistance as the jealous, envious patient proceeds to prove that the therapist is no more competent than the patient. Although patients often seek to idealize therapists, a reaction perhaps to their sense of personal neediness and helplessness, they often then proceed to take delight in demonstrating that their idol has clay feet.[8]

> The more the analyst's technique and behavior are suggestive of omniscience and omnipotence, the greater is the danger of a malignant form of regression. On the other hand, the more the analyst can reduce the inequality between his patient and himself, and the more unobtrusive and ordinary he can remain in his patient's eyes, the better are the chances of a benign form. . . .
>
> Michael Balint, 1968, p. 173

TAKING THE PATIENT SERIOUSLY: THE PLAUSIBILITY OF IDEAS

> [The] analyst's modesty must be no studied pose, but a reflection of the limitation of our knowledge.
>
> Sandor Ferenczi, 1928, p. 94

Patient ideas regarding what transpires between therapist and patient are to be seen as a hypothesis, and not a distortion of reality. What has led to their hypothesis must be explored. The therapist also has only a hypothesis regarding reality. A rigid posture of certainty by the therapist on what is transference and what is reality, on what the patient is *really* saying interferes with the patient's ability to self-reflect in a healthy manner. It is likely to be met with resistance.

Here-and-now work with the transference requires the therapist to take seriously the patient's viewpoint, not only to increase rapport, but because the patient is intelligent and perceptive. The therapist must honestly believe that the patient is a credible interpreter of his experience. Although these feelings may not always be accurate in an objective sense, in a subjective sense they create the patient's attitudes and influence future interactions.[9]

When attempting to interpret the transference in the here and now, it is helpful for the therapist to realize that the patient's understanding of the relationship is as plausible to the patient as he can make it. Reactions to the therapist are best understood in terms of what information the patient has about therapy and the therapist. It is helpful to realize that the patient is attempting to be as rational as he can given the narrow range of cues available in the therapeutic situation.[10] The patient's reaction makes sense to him in terms of what he experiences and perceives. His view of the relationship is always plausible if one takes the perspective of the patient.

When the therapist views the patient's attitudes in a spirit of seeing their possible plausibility in the light of what information the patient has, rather than in the spirit of either affirming or denying the patient's views, the way is open for further expression and elucidation of experience. Looking for what in the interaction has stirred up the patient's reactions, and viewing the patient's reactions as plausible given the patient's personal view of the situation, provides a foothold for the work of here-and-now transference analysis. In such work, it must be recognized that neither participant has a corner on the truth. Patient and therapist must engage in a give-and-take to work out an understanding that makes sense to both.

The impact of transference on the patient–therapist relationship is most effectively elucidated by a process in which the therapist interprets what is perceived and experienced while at the same time being receptive to the patient's interpretation of the process. The goal is not to define what is reality and how it is being distorted but rather what are the differing plausible ways in which they are perceiving the reality and how each is contributing to the other's perception.[11] This experience of attempting to mutually understand is often vastly different from what the patient typically elicits from others and can provide a curative experience in and of itself.[10]

As patient and therapist work toward understanding the underpinnings of the relationship, the opportunity presents itself to practice modifications that allow a more productive and mature interaction. The therapist and patient attempt to work out a relationship that is honest, genuine, and devoid of excess baggage from the past. The message to be conveyed in this work is that relationships are not conflict free, and that the therapist is willing to proceed, with openness and purpose, toward interpersonal conflict resolution. This stance implies a shift from the position of the observer to participant–observer—a shift from viewing the therapeutic encounter as objectively definable by the therapist to a view of the encounter as defined by the progressive elucidation of the manner in which the relationship is experienced by both participants.

Chapter Eleven

Premature Interpretation of Projection

When a neurotic patient meets a new object in ordinary life . . . . he will tend to project on to it his introjected archaic objects and the new object will become to that extent a phantasy object.

James Strachey, 1934, p. 139

Premature interpretation may be used defensively by the therapist unwilling to tolerate and contain the patient's projections and may serve as a retreat from the collaborative venture of examining here-and-now transference.

CONCERNS REGARDING PREMATURE INTERPRETATION OF PROJECTION

The therapist may obstruct effective work on transference analysis in the here and now by means of premature interpretation of the patient's transference projections. Analysis of transference in the here and now requires the therapist to assist the patient in examining his perceptions of the therapist, therapy, and their interaction. The therapist helps the patient gain an understanding of himself through an examination of his reactions to the therapist, and of the type of relationship developed as a result of these reactions. Patients project onto the therapist disowned feelings and attitudes as well as various internalized representations of self and object. Their reaction and interaction with the therapist is often strongly determined by their perception of these attributes now seen as residing within the therapist.

The therapist's interventions, however, need not be designed to force the patient to own these projections. The therapist may be too quick to interpret the patient's projections and to try to explain to the patient the real origin of his various feelings regarding the therapist. Such a stance by the therapist most often meets with defensiveness. The patient's ability to look at himself is compromised and made more difficult.

The therapist is ill-advised to force a patient to prematurely relinquish defenses that serve an important function in psychic organization. Epstein, in an excellent article on the management of transference projections, states that projection enables the patient's ego to avoid conflict by means of ridding itself of an element of experience that is dissonant with other elements of his self-image or self-perception.[1] Through projection an internal psychological conflict may be externalized. The conflict is no longer experienced as being between opposing aspects of the self, but rather between self and other, or self and one's environment. Although projection may create somewhat difficult, sometimes adversarial, relations between the person and whomever he projects unacceptable aspects of himself onto, such a stance, according to Epstein, has psychological survival value. Feelings are often projected becausethe patient cannot tolerate their ownership. By depositing elements of one's internal conflict in someone else, the person's beleaguered ego is better able to hold on to self-esteem and self-cohesion and to maintain an organization previously threatened by the prospect of inner conflict.

Premature interpretation of a patient's projections may complicate self-exploration in that the patient may experience the therapist's words as an assault that is unconsciously expected. The patient's initial projection of feelings and attitudes onto the therapist may be conceptualized as an intrusion by the patient into the therapist's life space. "Powered by powerful unconscious aggressive impulses, he has ejected something from within himself and forcibly injected it into the analyst, thereby violating the analyst's boundaries and vitiating his personhood, making of him an object of use."[2] The patient is felt to have unconscious awareness of the intrusive nature of the projection and to therefore expect a reciprocation or retribution in line with the *talion principle* (i.e., retaliation in kind). This unconscious intrusion and displacement onto the therapist creates within the patient's ego a state of paranoid expectation to receive a counterassault against his own inner life. What is said to the patient at such a moment, and how it is said, is crucial. A hasty transference interpretation informing the patient of how he is perceiving the therapist, what he is doing to the therapist, and why (in terms of his internal dynamics), is likely to be perceived by the patient's ready-to-be-persecuted ego as the expected and deserved counterassault.[1] This reaction is not likely to facilitate the openness necessary to use the interpretation, however accurate and insightful it may be.

Premature interpretive efforts are often the result of a pressure to respond or react which has been provoked by the patient's interpersonal stance vis-à-vis the therapist. By responding too quickly, the therapist may become an unwitting participant in a scenario that unconsciously externalizes the patient's internalized view of self and others, that is, the relationship between his internalized representations of himself and the world of objects. A repetition compulsion or validation of life script may be orchestrated. The patient with paranoid trends, for example, who feels unjustly treated by a hostile world, may unconsciously attempt to elicit a punitive reaction from the therapist. This punishment could take the form of telling the patient, at a point when the patient's ego is unable to cope with this knowledge, that the hostility attributed to others is really the projection of his own anger and "badness."

Another and related problem with premature interpretation of a patient's projection especially relates to situations in which the content of the projection (e.g., hostile, aggressive impulses) results in the therapist being viewed as potentially malevolent and untrustworthy. A patient currently experiencing the therapist in a negative light will often find it very difficult to trust what it is the therapist is saying. An interpretation from a "bad object" is likely to be rejected.

CAUSES OF PREMATURE INTERPRETATION

Premature interpretation of feelings the patient projects onto the therapist is often a defense against the affect stirred up within the therapist by these projections. The therapist may feel unable to tolerate and contain the feelings evoked by the projection, and by the patient's reaction to the therapist, as a result of the patient perceiving the projected attributes within the therapist. The therapist, for instance, may have difficulty being accused by the patient as incompetent, inferior, or inadequate—an accusation relating to the projection of the patient's own sense of inadequacy. "We may feel vitiated, controlled, and threatened and our own survival needs may impel us to rid ourselves of the patient's projections so that we can experience the relief of feeling ourselves again. And this is true whether the patient makes of us a devil or an angel."[3] In order to reestablish his sense of balance, equilibrium, and therapeutic comfort, the therapist may feel the urge to rid himself of the patient's projections through interpreting their origin. The act of interpreting at such moments may both be an unwitting acting out of the therapist's need to disown the unwanted projections and to attack the patient for what he is doing to him.[1]

Premature interpretation of projection may occur as an

attempt to relieve therapist anxiety of another sort. It is important to ascertain in work with projection whether interpretation is meant to promote growth and maturation, or to soothe our own anxieties and discomforts. With patients experiencing more serious psychological turmoil and disturbance, the desperate nature of their behaviors and the primitiveness and intensity of certain feelings, like hate and destruction, are a major test of the therapist's skill and patience.[4] When these feelings emerge, the therapist is vulnerable to the pressure to do something, to attempt to replace badness with goodness, hatred with love. The therapist must constantly be aware of the tendency to reduce personal anxiety and discomfort by means of a precipitous attempt to change the patient's feelings.

THE THERAPIST'S STANCE VIS-À-VIS PROJECTION

As noted earlier, the therapist is ill-advised to force a patient to prematurely relinquish projective defenses in that they often serve an important function in psychic organization. Kohut viewed the patient's use of projection as the first step toward tolerance of intrapsychic conflict. He cautions the therapist to avoid hasty interpretations of projection because through his projections, the patient is beginning to verbalize those aspects of himself which are conflictual and found unacceptable. Kohut felt that psychological change could begin by initially allowing the patient to express his conflicts by projecting them. The technique he found most useful to avoid rejecting the patient's perception was to repeat back what the patient said, a kind of echoing procedure.[5]

To successfully work with a patient's projection, the therapist must first contain the projection. That is, he must live with the feelings engendered in him without denying, acting upon, or in other ways attempting to dissociate himself from them. As discussed earlier, this can be a difficult task that is fraught with the potential for countertransference acting out. The therapist attempts to draw out the patient's feelings and to engage in a serious and nondefensive investigation of them. He is cautioned to initially restrict comments and questions to those that are directed away from the patient's ego and toward his own ego.

> If the patient, for instance, finds fault with the analyst or impugns his motives or intentions, the patient's perceptions and ideas should not be challenged; they should either be reflected — e.g., you mean, I am such-and-such a kind of person, or I'm really out to get you — or they should be objectively investigated: he can be asked, for example, to describe the analyst's faults more fully and asked for his ideas on how they should be corrected.[6]

The patient may be asked to share his ideas regarding the therapist's motives: whether they are conscious or unconscious. He may also be encouraged in nonthreatening fashion to discuss just how it was that he came to form his opinion regarding the therapist and perhaps to discuss the evidence he used. To briefly illustrate: a patient comes for therapy who has internalized a very critical and demanding image of the parental object. He subsequently becomes perfectionistic and demanding of himself, and suffers from depression. In therapy he projects this internalized representation of a disapproving parent onto the therapist and perceives the therapist as condemning, overly demanding, and unforgiving. He then relates in a fashion used to relate to the original parent: he becomes fearful and appeasing, yet stubborn and passively resistant. The therapist's task is to help the patient express his perceptions of the therapist, how these perceptions are developed, what they are based on, and how they may affect his subsequent reactions to the therapist. The therapist does not disown the patient's projections but seeks to discuss, study, and more clearly understand them. This stance seeks to detoxify unacceptable feelings, which ultimately allows the patient to integrate rather than defend against them.

The question of how much of that which the patient attributes to the therapist is distorted or reality based is treated as irrelevant. All of the patient's ideas and perceptions are taken seriously. What is necessary is a continuing elucidation of the patient's view of the therapeutic situation as an integral part of the process. The therapist's position that he is dealing with plausible hypotheses on the patient's part facilitates the discovery process.

The therapist's strategy in regard to managing projection is to draw out the patient's projection of his own insufficiencies until his ego is ready to take them back.[1] Premature interpretation of projection may induce a premature return of the patient's badness to his ego, with a resulting decrease in self-esteem. The therapist doesn't challenge the accuracy of the perception as much as continue to discuss it. Nor does he say anything in a defensive fashion which might invalidate the patient's negative feelings or judgments regarding him. This approach, according to Epstein, reduces paranoid anxiety because it steadily conveys reassurance that the therapist has been unharmed by the patient's projections and is more interested in understanding the patient than in counterattacking and punishing.

With a persevering, nondefensive discussion of the patient's perception, one hopes to draw out the patient's feelings, often of an aggressive and hostile nature, to deflect them away from the patient's ego and to gradually diffuse them. The ability of the therapist to tolerate the patient's projection of deficiencies and imperfections without having to defensively reject those feelings facilitates the patient's ability to gradually tolerate and contain his bad feelings without having to project them, turn them against the self, or convert them into symptoms.[1]

The above stance is meant to convey that the therapist (1) has a strong ego and is not harmed by the patient's projections, (2) has a desire to understand the patient's interpersonal and intrapsychic processes, and (3) is able to tolerate projections of unwanted (intolerable) aspects of the patient onto himself. Trust in the therapeutic process is communicated and the patient is helped to gradually tolerate aspects of oneself that were previously defended against by disavowal and projection.

It must be noted that while Epstein applies this approach to work with borderline patients, these principles are seen by the present author as valid for individuals of varied disturbance levels. The principle to be gleaned is that the patient cannot be too quickly pushed to tolerate attributes that, if owned, will lead to intolerable conflict. The therapist who, in reaction to his own anxiety, impatience, or need to be profound, requires the patient to reintegrate an aspect of himself when he is not capable of doing so, will severely compromise the patient–therapist collaboration.

Part IV

Technique of Dealing
with Transference

Chapter Twelve

Interpretation

What is ultimately of significance for the analytic process is not what the analyst says, or thinks he says, but what the patient experiences in connection with what the analyst says.

Paul and Anna Ornstein, 1985, p. 50

Much of here-and-now work, and dynamic therapy in general, involves talking to the patient about himself. It may be helpful to review how this task is accomplished, that is, the interpretive process.

VALUE OF INTERPRETATION

Interpretation may be viewed as explaining or giving meaning to an experience. This naming and clarification helps bring the patient's inner experiences out of the shadows, gives them shape, and permits the patient to draw upon his cognitive powers for aid in adaptation.[1] The therapist interprets when he believes that he has some understanding that the patient can't discern or organize without help.[2] When the patient is explaining himself to the therapist, or to himself, without difficulty, there is no need for interpretation.

Interpretation aids in the laying down and integration of internal structure. The understanding and explaining of the patient's inner state leads to the "transmuting internalization" of the therapist and his function, and to the acquisition of psychic structure.[3] Providing an understanding of the nature and development of the patient's needs without actually fulfilling these needs is viewed as an optimal frustration; the patient is empathically held yet challenged to continue his growth and maturation by doing for himself that which he wishes the therapist–parent to do for him.

The term *interpretation* may be an inaccurate and potentially misleading term for what the therapist actually does.[4] It may inappropriately imply a magical reading of a crystal ball through which an unconscious, underlying meaning is deciphered by the therapist and conveyed to the patient. Interpretation is more helpfully thought of as a collaborative attempt to further the patient's self-understanding through explanation, restructuring, and feedback regarding his intrapsychic and interpersonal processes. Increased interest in the patient's defensive organization has led to a greater focus on the process and method of providing interpretations.[5]

PRINCIPLES REGARDING INTERPRETATION

A number of maxims may be gleaned from a review of the clinical and theoretical writing on interpretation. These include such time-proven guidelines as: "prepare the patient," "surface before depth," "defense before what is being defended against," "make ego-dystonic what is ego-syntonic," "be timely," "avoid theoretical jargon," and "use the patient's idiom."

Interpretations are most effective when they are concrete, specific, and detailed to fit the individual situation. When the therapist embarks upon a general theme, interpretations cannot always avoid being vague, but it is necessary to eventually dovetail one's observations with the specifics of the patient's life situation.[6] Global accusations such as the determination that someone is "narcissistic," "dependent," or "passive–aggressive" are likely to be met with resistance. No person is the same in all situations. To apply a global term is incongruent with significant aspects of the person.[7]

Unless there is a clear reason for being a bit subtle and obscure, interpretations are best when they are simple, direct, and clear.[8] If possible, it is useful to help the patient to see how the therapist came up with the observation. This enables the patient to learn a means of thinking about data, makes the therapist less mysterious and more easily emulated, and encourages the patient to think for himself.

The best interpretations have strong supporting arguments, are consonant with the patient's frame of reference, and have generalizability.[7] Interpretations are bolstered by empirical observations. Prior to offering an interpretation, the therapist must decide whether the information being used to base his interpretation is reasonably sound. It is important when interpreting for both patient and therapist to be aware of what specifically is being commented upon. In regard to here-and-now transference analysis, for example, the interpretation should be preceded by establishing between patient and therapist as clearly as possible the actual behavior sequence that is being examined. Failure to do so may result in patient and therapist talking about different things.

In addition to helping the patient attain greater awareness and more in-depth understanding of areas of conflict and ego dysfunction, it is advantageous for the therapist to aid the patient in developing awareness of his strengths and areas of sound functioning. It may be just be as important for the patient to become aware of the ways in which he copes, as well as the ways in which he is anxious or ineffectual.[9] For some patients, their global condemnation of themselves as neurotic or a failure obscures significant islands of ego strength and productive functioning that could be built upon. An additional benefit in identifying strengths is that the patient will weather the more difficult and frustrating times best if he feels that the therapist can respect and find the good in him.[10]

Thus, we are told that if we interpret too soon or too rashly, we run the risk of losing a patient; that unless we interpret promptly and deeply we run the risk of losing a patient; that interpretation may give rise to intolerable and unmanageable outbreaks of anxiety by "liberating" it; that interpretation is the only way of enabling a patient to cope with an unmanageable outbreak of anxiety by "resolving" it; that interpretations must always refer to material on the very point of emerging into consciousness; that the most useful interpretations are really deep ones; "Be cautious with your interpretations!" says one voice; "When in doubt, interpret!" says another. Nevertheless, although there is evidently a good deal of confusion in all of this, I do not think these views are necessarily incompatible; the various pieces of advice may turn out to refer to different circumstances and different cases and to imply different uses of the word "interpretation."

James Strachey, 1934, pp. 141–142.

FRUGALITY AND PARSIMONY

The supply of interpretations, like that of advice, greatly exceeds the need for them.

H.S. Sullivan, 1947, p. 92

Parsimony and frugality are to be favored with regard to interpretations. In the optimal world the therapist gives the patient the least amount of help needed and focuses his energy less on startling revelation, and more on instigating the patient's interest in discovering for himself the meaning of his behavior.

Interpretations should be made only when the patient cannot achieve this discovery. The therapist's ultimate task is to permit and encourage the patient to treat himself in the therapist's presence much as one might allow a child to play in his parents' presence, or a musician to practice in the presence of his teacher.[11] The patient's ability to view the therapy as his own decreases resistance to process and facilitates his assuming responsibility for what occurs in his therapy and, ultimately, in his life.

Too much help with interpretation decreases the internal incentive of the patient and fosters passivity. The omniscient and omnipotent therapist invites magical fantasies. Patients' autonomy and initiative, developed through the struggle of trial, effort, and eventual mastery, are too easily curtailed by the too good, too able, too helpful therapist.[12] A further benefit of being frugal with interpretations: numerous interpretive efforts by the therapist may impel the patient, already feeling inadequate and "one-down," to feel further put down by the all-knowing and powerful therapist. Feelings regarding the "haves" and "have-nots" may develop, which may be followed by intense envy. This envy may be acted out through increased resistance, defensiveness, and in extreme cases, destruction and spoiling of the therapy.[13]

A most helpful goal for therapist intervention is to assist the patient to integrate one step beyond his present awareness. Encouraging the patient to increase his understanding through his own efforts may elicit from the patient such comments as "I can't" or "I don't know." The therapist may respond to such a statement with the brief, encouraging intervention of "Try." This simple, ego-building response is, according to Blanck and Blanck, more than encouragement. It gently refuses to do the therapeutic work for the patient, so that he may gain confidence in his own ability "instead of remaining fixated in admiration of a brilliant therapist who makes interpretations that he, the patient, could never match."[14]

There is no magic in the particular choice of words used when interpreting. More important is the therapist's attitude and emotional set. Interpretations are often best when made tentatively and in question form. Interpretations of a hypothetical nature, beginning with such phrases as "Is it possible that . . . ," or "Could it be that . . . ," offer the patient an opportunity to reflect and work with the material. The patient has the opportunity to agree or disagree, or to further the line of thought through correction, amendment, or addition.[15] Interpretations are best offered, not forced. The therapist invites the patient to reflect, to consider and become curious, and to engage in collaborative inquiry.

> An interpretation should rarely go as far as possible. It should, by preference, fall short even of its immediate intended goal. This gives the patient an opportunity to extend your interpretation, gives him a greater share in the proceedings, and will mitigate to some extent the trauma of being the victim of your help. . . .
>
> Sidney Tarachow, 1963, p. 49

TIMING

> When you have found the right interpretation, another task lies ahead. You must wait for the right moment at which you can communicate your interpretation to the patient with some prospect of success. . . . You will be making a bad mistake if . . . you throw your interpretations at the patient's head as soon as you have found them.
>
> Sigmund Freud, 1926, p. 220

The timing of interpretations is considered to be an essential component of dynamic technique. Freud cautions the therapist to avoid offering the patient an interpretation of a symptom, or the translation of a wish, until the patient is already so close to it that he has only one short step more to make in order to get hold of the explanation for himself.[16]

For the patient with a reasonably intact and well-defended ego, the most effective time for interpretation is when the conflictual issue is active, bubbling over, and the patient is experiencing immediate affective discomfort linked to this issue.[1] Interpretations are best assimilated when they are given when the patient is an optimal distance from the affect associated with the events being interpreted. An interpretation cannot be given while the patient is overwhelmed by emotional reactions. Reactions of acute mourning, for example, are not subject to interpretation. Conversely, when the patient's affect in the present moment is too far removed from the conflict the therapist seeks to examine, its interpretation will have minimal effect.

The present state of the patient–therapist relationship must be taken into account when assessing the correct timing of the interpretation. Prior to a potentially unwelcome interpretation, the therapist needs to ascertain whether the patient's trust and confidence in him is sufficient to tolerate the strain.[17] Interpretation is best received when a strong therapeutic alliance is present. An interpretation made within the framework of a chronic, persistent negative transference is not likely to be assimilated. The experience of the therapist as a punitive, threatening object will elicit defensiveness, making it difficult for the patient to process any observations that are offered at that moment. This is especially true when the therapist is *actually* angry with the patient; an interpretation at such a time will likely fall upon an unreceptive patient who, in part, may ration-alize whatever is said as the therapist's anger doing the talking.

The therapist may hold on to interpretation too long. Such behavior may result in either a missed opportunity as the patient proceeds to another topic, or, as in the case of a transference interpretation, the affect built up in the patient (love or hostility) may reach a point where he will no longer heed what the therapist has to say.[18] On the other hand, a hasty interpretation made before the patient is ready may increase the defensiveness and tenacity with which he maintains certain beliefs. It must be remembered that one's defenses, albeit constricting and painful, serve a purpose in the patient's psychological economy. They are to be approached respectfully and should not be stripped away without thought.

Another concern with an early, premature interpretation: such an intervention may provide premature closure and close the patient down.[12] Having been provided an explanation, however hasty, the patient may cease verbalizing. This may compromise the patient's opportunity to more deeply explore his feelings and to share what is most painful, grievous, or anxiety-provoking.

What countertransference difficulties underlie the hasty, premature interpretation? Sederer and Thorbeck posit that hasty interpretations by the therapist are often a reaction to his own difficulty in understanding and containing the patient's feelings. Interpretations, according to this view, may be offered as much to relieve tension in the therapist as to further the patient. The patient's pain may thus stir up anxiety and the pressure toward action to relieve this anxiety. "At [such] moments interpretations are like sedatives; they quiet people down but do not help to heal the wounds. They help us professionals to feel potent at a time when we would otherwise recognize the limits of our role."[19]

It is not difficult for a skilled analyst to read the patient's secret wishes plainly between the lines of his complaints and the story of his illness; but what a measure of self-complacency and thoughtlessness must be possessed by anyone who can, on the shortest acquaintance, inform a stranger who is entirely ignorant of all the tenets of analysis that he is attached to his mother by incestuous ties, that he harbours wishes for the death of his wife whom he appears to love, that he conceals an intention of betraying his superior and so on! I have heard that there are analysts who plume themselves upon these kinds of lightning diagnoses and "express" treatments, but I must warn everyone against following such examples. Behavior of this sort will completely discredit oneself and the treatment in the patient's eyes and will arouse the most violent opposition in him . . . the therapeutic effect will be nil; but the deterring of the patient from analysis will be final.

Sigmund Freud, 1913, p. 140

Chapter Thirteen

Working Through

Much as we would like it otherwise, psychotherapy is . . . a long, lumbering process in which the same issues are repeatedly worked through in the therapy environment and are tested and retested in the patient's life environment.

Irvin Yalom, 1980, pp. 307–308

Insight alone has no magical qualities.

Paul Dewald, 1964, p. 245

Here-and-now work focuses on interpretation of transference material as a means of furthering intrapsychic understanding and interpersonal learning. Increases in insight and understanding, however, don't automatically yield significant personality change and growth; this requires adherence to the process of working through.

DEFINITIONS AND OVERVIEW

The concept of working through was initially discussed by Freud in his (1914) paper "Remembering, Repeating, and Working Through." In this paper he noted that beginners in analytic practice were inclined to believe that the interpretation of resistance would lead to its cessation. Young analysts often complained that even though they had pointed out the patient's resistance, no change occurred; indeed, the resistance often became stronger. In commenting on such situations

Freud stressed patience and continued perseverance. He wrote that

> giving resistance a name could not result in its immediate cessation. One must allow the patient time to become more conversant with the resistance with which he has now become acquainted, to work through it . . . the doctor has nothing else to do than to wait and let things take their course, a course which cannot be avoided or always hastened . . . The working through of the resistances may in practice turn out to be an arduous task for the subject of the analysis and a trial of patience for the analyst. Nevertheless it is a part of the work which effects the greatest changes in the patient . . .[1]

Fenichel echoes Freud's comments, stating that successful interpretive work "is not a single operation resulting in a single abreaction; it is, rather, a chronic process of working through, which shows the patient again and again the same conflicts and his usual way of reacting to them, but from new angles and in new connections."[2] The therapist is thus encouraged to assist the patient in a careful exploration of his problem in all its myriad forms. Let us take, for example, a problem with authority. The patient could be assisted in viewing how this particular conflict may express itself in a variety of different manners in the session. These expressions could range from outright opposition to the therapist, where the patient reflexively responds in a contrary fashion; to more subtle control struggles, the patient striving to provide sound, rational argument which gently "one-ups" the therapist; to a relatively passive, submissive stance, with the patient automatically agreeing with therapist observations with little thought or reflection.

In addition to exploring how a specific conflict may be expressed in a variety of fashions, the working through concept suggests that the patient be assisted in viewing this conflict from different perspectives or vantage points. The patient could be helped to view the impact of his behavior through the eyes of those he interacts with. It is productive for him to learn how others typically feel when they are with him, how such feelings impact their reactions to him, and how their reactions to him in turn may affect his feelings regarding himself. Initially done between patient and therapist, such exploration may be gradually expanded to significant individuals in his daily life. To illustrate:

> A patient (AB) presented for therapy to work on problems with self-esteem, loneliness and depression. In the course of therapy it appeared that therapist comments and observations were often inordinately painful for AB. The therapist began to feel like he was walking on eggs. He found himself backing off and treating her gingerly. Following supervisory consultation the therapist offered his observations of this interaction pattern. AB responded with hurt, then anger as she felt criticized. Further discussion, however, allowed her to increase awareness of how she responded to the therapist, and indeed to others as well. She was somewhat surprised to learn that her sensitivity to other people's comments to her often led them to be reluctant to interact with her in an open, honest, free-flowing manner. The reactions of others, in turn, had a significant effect on her feelings about herself. Feeling avoided and not valued by others, she struggled to value herself.

While helping a patient examine one facet of behavior in all its various means of expression, one must be sensitive to the realization that behavior elements are interlocked.[3] Work on one facet of behavior will lead to another which must receive focus and attention. This, in turn, will lead to other interlocking facets. The therapist must be able to appreciate interrelatedness of behavior and be able to understand a particular reaction within the greater mosaic that makes up the patient's overall psychological organization. One is cautioned to avoid viewing a specific behavioral dynamic as existing as a separate entity, unrelated to other aspects of the patient's psychology. For instance, work on the authority conflict discussed earlier will, in all likelihood, lead to work on the patient's issues regarding need for control, perfectionism, and fear of failure. The relationship of these issues with each other, as well as with the other aspects of the patient's personality, will often need to be elucidated before significant change may occur. "It is not possible to change only one or two facets of this chain. The entire chain must change in order for the patient's experience of living to become significantly improved."[4]

PRACTICING

Working through was originally applied to the tedious process of overcoming the patient's resistance to the treatment process — in particular, to the uncovering of painful and anxiety-provoking insights. Marmor observed that ego-oriented analysts are increasingly applying this concept to the equally laborious task of overcoming the patient's resistance to actual behavioral change. He writes that

> neither insights, nor confrontations, nor transference interpretations in and of themselves, necessarily produce fundamental change, although occasionally we may be gratified to see change occur only on that basis. More often than not . . . we find it necessary, sooner or later . . . gently and persistently to begin to encourage the patient to come to grips directly with the anxiety-provoking situation, and by a series of graduated successes eventually to achieve the desired sense of mastery.[5]

This mastery of conflictual, self-defeating behavior often first occurs by means of practice with the therapist in their here-and-now relationship. As the patient gains an awareness of his manner of relating to the therapist, of what brings about this relationship pattern, as well as what its consequences are, the opportunity to behave in a different fashion is made possible. The patient is offered use of the therapeutic interaction to practice new and more satisfactory means of behaving. The patient may practice new behavior and then follow up with an examination of his experience. Feelings before and after the new behavior may be explored. What, for example, were the anxieties prior to the risk of behaving differently? These may be explored in relation to expectations regarding the therapist. The patient's reactions during and immediately after practicing may be elucidated. This is often a mixture of anxiety concerning the feared consequences, relief that it is over, and a nascent sense of accomplishment. Repeated practice and processing of this practice promotes subsequent mastery.

Conflict resolution in the here and now provides an important model as well as tools for resolution of conflict in the patient's outside life. As the patient practices a new means of interacting with the therapist, it is important to assist the patient in applying what has been learned in the patient–therapist relationship to the patient's outside relations. It is not enough that the therapist see the patient as dealing with the therapist in a different fashion. Discipline and perseverance are needed to help the patient follow through on changing his behavior with others. This follow-through is often needed to counteract the possibility that the patient may behave differently in the safe environment of therapy but fail to generalize these changes to his living situation.

DIFFICULTIES IN INDUCING CHANGE

> *Experience has taught us that psychoanalytic therapy – the liberation of a human being from his neurotic symptoms, inhibitions and abnormalities of character – is a lengthy business.*
>
> Sigmund Freud, 1937, p. 373

During the working-through process the therapist strives to aid the patient in translating what has been learned about himself into emotional growth and behavioral change. This can be a forbidding process. Freud thought the difficulty in the working through to be related to the patient's resistance to giving up unconscious, archaic wishes.[6] The patient was viewed as striving to hold onto the hope that certain childhood longings would be fulfilled. The patient, according to Freud, often unconsciously behaved in a fashion so as to replicate childhood relationships in order to provide an opportunity for these longings to be gratified. Freud felt that insight into this process was unconsciously perceived by the patient as impeding this process and therefore resisted. Changes in behavior would thus threaten the patient's attempt to get present objects to provide what is longed for from childhood objects.

The resistance to giving up childhood longings is but one possible reason that working through is difficult. Persistent modes of thinking and feeling are reinforced in important ways by the consequences of the patient's day-to-day actions in living.[7] A person's distrust for others, for instance, may result in a manner of relating (e.g., guardedness, defensiveness) that actually creates a malevolent or rejecting environment, leading to further guarded, defensive behavior. By behaving in a particular fashion, a person may actually create an environment that provides continued validation for the behavioral stance that supports his original premise.

Even with an effective therapy through which the patient learns to avoid continually creating conditions that support his internal suppositions, change still comes hard. A considerable working through may be necessary because the disconfirming experience with the therapist is at odds with a long series of experiences that have produced expectations not readily relinquished after just one or two disconfirmations.[8]

Generalization of change from therapy to one's outside life is additionally difficult because abandoning familiar ways of relating to others produces anxiety until new patterns are developed. In one's outside relations there is often pressure by significant others to maintain one's present style of relating. This often complements the other, or at least is something that they are used to. Significant pressure may be brought to bear on the patient to remain the same.

> *There are many environments where a more positive emergence of the patient would be destroyed by the collective action of others who needed him to stay the same for the sake of system stability.*
>
> James Gustafson, 1986, p. 87

OVERCOMING RESISTANCE TO CHANGE

In the working through, the therapist helps the patient look at his resistance to using insight into his defensive structure and interpersonal style for behavioral change. Yalom offers some helpful considerations on overcoming patient resistance to change:[9]

1. *Responsibility*. The therapist helps the patient work toward accepting responsibility for whatever changes are to occur

in his life. He must become cognizant that a) others will not change *for* him b) change will not occur *to* him, and c) *he* holds sole responsibility for what he chooses to make of his future.

2. *Danger in Change.* The fear of change is often a productive focus. The assumption may be safely made that the patient is afraid of change. The therapist attempts to clarify and then detoxify the fear. One may appeal to the patient's reason and cognitive powers. Naming and identifying the fear, in the process developing some intellectual rationale and mastery, may lead to its decrease. In addition, the patient may be encouraged to face the fear in carefully calibrated doses, initially with the therapist, later with others.

3. *What Do You Really Want?* The patient must realize that to get what he really wants, he must change. Neurotic behavior sabotages realizations of mature goals and needs while partially satisfying other, more infantile ones. The patient must be helped to choose among conflicting alternatives and to relinquish those goals which can't be fulfilled except at great loss to his integrity and autonomy.

4. *Sense of Potency.* The patient must be aided to develop the sense that change is possible and that he has the ability to accomplish it. Yalom suggests the use of interpretation and provision of an explanatory framework as a means of increasing one's potency. Providing an explanation and meaning to his behavior helps the patient feel a sense of mastery. Explanation is viewed as providing an order for life, placing it in a more coherent and predictable pattern which offers the patient a greater sense of control over himself.

From a here-and-now perspective, the patient's sense of potency may be enhanced by the experience of progressively modifying his relationship with the therapist in a more constructive and mature direction. The ability to productively impact the here-and-now relationship between patient and therapist promotes confidence in the patient's ability to change his means of interaction in other relationships.

Chapter Fourteen

Resolution

*Transference analysis is the slow and painful experi-
ence of clearing the ground of left-overs from past
experience, both in transference and counter-trans-
ference, so that therapist and patient can at last meet
"mentally face to face" and know that they know each
other as two human beings. This is without doubt the
most important kind of relationship of which human
beings are capable and it is not to be confused with
erotic "falling in love."*

Harry Guntrip, 1969, p. 353

Analysis of transference in the here and now assists the patient in resolving psychological conflict and its ensuing interpersonal manifestation. The following concepts are deemed important in this process: (1) the new discovery of objects through analyzing obstacles to new means of viewing and relating to others, (2) the experience of beneficial uncertainty induced through having one's behavior responded to with concern and attempts at understanding rather than neurotic engagement, and (3) the ability of the patient to learn responsibility for the creation of his world.

A NEW DISCOVERY OF OBJECTS

Once we see the world differently, we seem to inhabit a different world.

Arnold Goldberg, 1985, p. 64

Here-and-now work attempts to foster a new experience of relating. This is not done through a manipulation of the transference to create a corrective emotional experience, but rather through a systematic working through and resolution of transference material to reach a new experience of self and others. Analysis of transference in the here and now opens the way to new object relations through a step-by-step removal of impediments to such relations as represented by the transference. The identification and working through of transference distortions and resulting interpersonal conflicts allow the therapist to become available as a new object leading to a new way of relating to others and to oneself. An important aspect of this process is the ability of the therapist to facilitate the patient's ability to experience relationships in a different manner than before. What is stressed is the new discovery of objects, not the discovery of new objects.[1] As the patient is able to understand and work through distortions resulting from transference attitudes, he begins to see others starting with the therapist, in a new way.

The therapist aims to facilitate the patient's view of the therapist as a person with legitimate strengths and weaknesses, as opposed to a product of his projections. Development of a more realistic view of the therapist applies to the patient's idealizing tendencies as well as the projection of bad object representations. To transfer is to generalize in relatively unquestioning terms.[2] This disregards the therapist as he actually is and presses him into a mold which violates his reality. To distort another person through idealization is by no means less problematic than to invest him with diabolic tendencies. In either case, his personality is disregarded and attacked. Whether the therapist serves as a receptacle for a bad or good object representation, it still reflects the patient's stance: "I have figured you out without bothering to learn who you are and I shall deal with you on the assumption that you have no individuality. I shall apply my stereotyped patterns of understanding to you just as I apply them to others."[3]

The goal of here-and-now work is to establish more realistic object relations, first with the therapist, then with others. The therapist strives to help the patient develop a more successful interaction within the therapy relationship than was experienced in the past. A focus on transference is intended to remove obstacles which interfere with the patient's ability to deal with the therapist in a relatively mature, rational, and nonconflictual manner. If transference is a preexisting perceptual and emotional bias, resolution of the transference helps the patient add flexibility and decrease constriction to the manner in which the therapeutic situation is viewed. The therapist and patient attempt to work out a relationship that is a realistic reflection of the present and devoid of excess baggage from the past. The message to be conveyed is that relationships are not conflict-free, and that the therapist is willing to proceed, with openness and purpose, toward resolution of conflict with others.

BENEFICIAL UNCERTAINTY

Here-and-now work aids in transference resolution in that the very act of examining his interactions provides a new experience for the patient.[4] The patient assumes that his behavior will result in certain predictable responses from the therapist, responses that have been elicited many times in the past from many different people. Relying on past learning, the patient unconsciously attempts to elicit behavior and recreate situations with the therapist that resonate with his internalized experiences of the world. By examining and not reacting, thereby dealing differently than others have, the therapist offers a new experience to the patient. A potentially valuable uncertainty is induced as the patient's coping strategies are not reinforced.[5] Initially puzzling, often frustrating, and anxiety-provoking, this experience contains within it the possibility for the patient to gain understanding of the inappropriateness of past reaction and to practice change. Thus, Freebury writes that the therapist's ability to listen and to empathically communicate his understanding leads to a unique interpersonal experience which is discordant with anything the patient has experienced before. The newness of this experience may cause the patient to attempt to remove this discordance by provoking the therapist to respond as others have done in the past. If this fails, it becomes necessary for the patient to revise long-held maladaptive beliefs about self and other. "It is the therapist's ability to avoid such repetition that promises something different and gives rise to hope. It is this hope that sustains both patient and therapist in the face of the often painful work."[6]

Of critical importance in the provision of new experience is the process of reflection and examination of the experience, as opposed to merely not reinforcing past behavior. The role of new experience, and the role of new experience that is reflected upon and examined, are different. The latter is viewed as effective, the former less so.[7]

RESPONSIBILITY

Here-and-now transference analysis offers an effective medium to increase patients' awareness of their responsibility for the quality and variety of interactions they become involved in. A goal of this work is to help patients see that the responsibility of their experience of relationship lies primarily with themselves.[8] It is helpful for the therapist to work from the frame of reference that patients create their own distress.[9] It is not chance, or bad luck or bad genes that have caused a patient to be lonely, isolated, chronically abused, or insomniac. The therapist must ascertain what role patients play in their own dilemmas, and communicate this insight. Motivation for change is very intimately associated with the ability to see how one is involved in creating one's world. "If one continues to believe that distress is caused by others, by bad luck, by an unsatisfying job—in short, by something outside oneself—why invest energy in personal change? In the face of such a belief system, the obvious strategy is not therapeutic but activist: to change one's environment."[10]

The therapist uses the here and now to aid patients in identifying and comprehending the nature of their behavior and its impact on others. Patients learn how their typical means of loving, hating, and attempting to get what they want, affect the reactions of others to them and, in turn, their feelings about themselves. They learn how they are drawn to recreate, with current objects, the battles being unconsciously waged with their internal objects. If effectively done, patients less and less present themselves as governed by impulses, defenses, and conflicts and more and more as the authors of their existence. "Even when all the necessities or terrible happenings of their past and present existences have been taken into account, patients come to realize how much has always depended on what they have made of these factors, whether they be family constellations, traumas, infirmities, losses, or sexual anatomy."[11]

The patient begins therapy expecting much from the therapist. Through wise counsel, the therapist is expected to supply the key for changing one's life, one's relations with people, one's performance on the job . . . the list could go on. Yet what does the therapist do? He questions and explores, he points out and provides feedback. He helps the patient learn about himself, how he became this person, and what he does to maintain this identity. Such a focus on his intrapsychic and interpersonal processes is enlightening, yet the patient inevitably suffers a certain disappointment and disillusionment. The patient seeks magic but receives observations on how he creates and sustains his existence, how he is the agent of his own life. The therapist's main contribution comes in helping the patient realize this.

Wishing for solutions from omniscient others, the patient learns—somewhat reluctantly—that the most effective solutions come from within. This learning experience is a loss of a sort, a narcissistic blow. The patient loses the illusion that there exists a parental figure who'll make everything right, and the therapist loses the opportunity to be one. Such losses are most difficult and may lead to resistances from both patient and therapist.

> One priceless thing the patient learns in therapy is the limits of relationship. One learns what one can get from others but, perhaps even more important, one learns what one cannot get from others.
>
> Irvin Yalom, 1980, pp. 406-407

Chapter Fifteen

Considerations in Implementing a Here-and-Now Approach

I think I am well-advised, however, to call these rules "recommendations" and not to claim any unconditional acceptance for them. The extraordinary diversity of the psychical constellations concerned, the plasticity of all mental processes and the wealth of determining factors oppose any mechanization of the technique.

Sigmund Freud, 1913 p. 123

It is hoped that perusal of this text will sensitize the therapist to the value of a here-and-now focus as well as aid him in exploring the resistances inherent in this focus. As the therapist pays greater attention to this aspect of the therapeutic process, it is important to be aware of the tendency to overemphasize what one may feel has been previously underemphasized. Interpretation of transference in general, and the here-and-now focus in specific, are but part of the therapist's armamentarium. Use of the here and now should not become a gimmick, nor should it be applied in rote and mechanical fashion. Such a stance courts numerous dangers. These include the following.

PREOCCUPATION WITH THERAPY

Exclusive interest by the therapist in the nature of the patient–therapist relationship may lead the patient to become preoccupied with the therapist and the here-and-now experience. The discussion and analysis of their relationship may take on exaggerated importance, with other aspects of the patient's life being unattended to. A comfortable, narcissistically gratifying experience of processing and reprocessing each other's reactions and feelings may be substituted for grappling with the troubling issues in the patient's life. An artificial separation between the patient's therapy and outside life may develop, with the former having little influence on the latter. A prolonged treatment often results as the gratification obtained in the transference relationship outweighs the patient's desire for change.

A related complication: those patients struggling with the neurotic need to ingratiate and gain the therapist's favor are often very sensitive to what behavior will please the therapist. A rigid focus on the here-and-now relationship informs the patient of what topics and information interest the therapist. This may compel the patient to concentrate here in order to gain the therapist's approval. The patient may end up discussing topics he feels are of importance to the therapist rather than what is important to him. In a subtle, sometimes not-so-subtle manner, the onus and responsibility of therapy become shifted to the therapist.

MISUSE OF TRANSFERENCE

Overemphasis on here-and-now phenomena may heighten the patient's emotional experience of the transference relationship in such a way that the patient: (1) may feel converted to the therapist's beliefs in evangelistic fashion, (2) upon experiencing the therapist as behaving diametrically different toward him than early significant others (e.g., the caring therapist versus indifferent parent), a corrective emotional experience may be achieved in which attitudes and beliefs are modified without the benefit of insight. There are dangers to both occurrences. In the former, the patient exchanges one parental dictum for another, often with an increasing rigidity of personality. In the latter, the effects of the corrective emotional experience tend to be shallow and short lived unless the patient is engaged in a working through process. Sole focus on here-and-now experience may also impede the process of generalizing what is learned within the therapeutic relationship to outside relations.

IMPAIRED ATTENTION

Undue focus on the here and now may skew the therapist's approach to patient material, robbing him of his multifaceted stance in listening (i.e., his evenly suspended attention). Freud teaches that as soon as the therapist concentrates attention to a certain degree, he begins to selectively attend to material.[1] As he begins to look for or be alert to certain aspects of the patient's presentation, his awareness of the total picture may be lost.

The therapist may concentrate his attention on the patient's transference behavior to such a degree that he fails to attend to other aspects of the patient's experience (e.g., an endogenous depression). By listening solely for the patient's reaction to the therapist, and by relating all thoughts and feelings back to the therapeutic relationship, the therapist courts the danger of failing to attain an appreciation and empathy for the patient's life as a whole.

THE THERAPIST OVERGENERALIZES

A final caveat regarding the here-and-now focus. The therapist may incorrectly assume that the patient's behavior in therapy accurately reflects the totality of his interpersonal relationships. This may result in a treatment based on overgeneralized observations and a less than adequate understanding of the patient's functioning. Behavior is complexly determined. It is, in part, a function of the situation the person finds himself in as well as the particular relationship he has to people within that situation. The therapist must be cognizant that the patient may not always show all aspects of himself to the therapist. Observation of the patient's transference behavior is but one avenue of understanding. Because some aspects of his functioning cannot be reproduced in the relationship to the therapist, knowledge of the patient's outside life often provides indispensable data for understanding of complexities of the patient's psychic functioning.[2]

What the patient does with the therapist may differ in important ways from how the patient relates to other significant individuals within his life. One assumes a continuity of behavior and we base much of our psychodynamic technique on this continuity; however, one must avoid the assumption that intra-session behavior perfectly mirrors extra-session relations.

WHEN TO BE CAUTIOUS ABOUT HERE-AND-NOW WORK

When does one focus attention on the here-and-now patient–therapist relationship and when does the therapist work in other areas of the therapeutic process? It is my experience that the here-and-now work resembles the gestalt "figure–ground" phenomenon. At some point it becomes the figure, the center of attention that is discussed, explored, and worked on; and at another point it acts as the ground, not focused on or attended to, but always there. Although it is difficult to explicitly delineate when to focus on the here and now, some observations are offered.

PRODUCTIVITY OF PATIENT FOCUS

In 1913, Freud recommended that so long as the patient's communications run on without obstruction, the theme of transference (i.e., a focus on the patient–therapist relationship), should be left untouched.[3] He later suggested that the therapist need not focus on the transference so long as it operates in favor of the joint work of analysis, but attention must be given to it if it becomes a resistance to the communication process.[4] Much can be gleaned from these comments regarding Freud's feelings about early interpretation of transference and his distinction between the obstructing and facilitating transference. More pertinent, however, for the present discussion is Freud's principle that so long as the patient is making productive use of the therapeutic process, so long as the patient is earnestly working to talk about himself and to explore and understand his feelings, introduction of a here-and-now focus is less of a priority. The patient–therapist relationship remains in the background; it becomes the ground. Comments directed at the here-and-now relationship at such a point are distracting and would be better kept until productive self-engagement is less evident. When the patient's communications become constricted, when allusions to the relationship become evident, and when the therapist begins to understand the self-defeating components of the patient's interpersonal strategies as they are being reenacted in the present, the patient–therapist relationship becomes the attention point, the figure, with all else receding into the background.

PATIENT RAPPORT

A trusting attachment and bond must be established with the patient before one discusses issues that might create anxiety and insecurity. Freud recommends that communications regarding transference be withheld until proper rapport has been developed with the patient.[3] Although it has been effectively argued that transference interpretations must often precede the establishment of trust with certain patients,[5] in most cases Freud's adage may be used to decide when a here-and-now focus may be productive.

Here-and-now interpretations are often best withheld until the patient develops a certain degree of trust and comfort with the therapist and the therapy. Interpretations of the patient's intrapsychic and interpersonal process will stir up a variety of reactions; there may be anxiety in that his way of being is called into question; the patient may feel criticized, ashamed or humiliated. Anger may result from narcissistic injury. The patient may feel a sense of loss and disappointment in that an interpretation, in a sense, deprives him of something: his fantasies, his defenses, his gratifications. Interpretation may also cause a sense of aloneness in that the act of interpreting requires the therapist, at least for that moment, to give up his empathic attachment, and to make a dispassionate observation.[6] The effects of interpretation are compounded when the communication is about the here-and-now relationship. Sullivan was very aware of the anxiety engendered by commenting on the patient–therapist relationship, stating that "it is difficult for most people to be straightforward and forthright in discussing their feelings, thoughts, impulses, and so on, with respect to a person with whom they are in the peculiar relationship of patient to a psychiatrist."[7] Because of this, Sullivan's exploratory work often was initially concerned with current events outside the treatment relationship and only gradually would he begin to focus on the current therapeutic relationship between doctor and patient.

IMPORTANT CURRENT EVENTS

The here-and-now focus is also contraindicated when the patient is assailed by a critical occurrence in his outside life. Events such as the death of a loved one, a tragic accident, or loss of a job, threaten one's sense of security and stability, and require a significant degree of psychic energy to manage. In such situations the patient must often use the majority of his energy to keep psychologically afloat. There is little incentive or motivation to use the therapy as a social microcosm in order to learn about how one typically behaves. A here-and-now focus during such times of stress will be felt as an unempathic assault to one's ego integrity.

Endnotes

Preface

1 S. Ferenczi, 1921

Chapter 1 Overview

 1 S. Freud, 1912a
 2 R. Greenson, 1967
 3 L. Stone, 1961, p. 42
 4 O. Fenichel, 1941
 5 F. Alexander, 1946
 6 D. Malan, 1963
 7 D. Malan, 1976
 8 H. Strupp and J. Binder, 1984
 9 G. Bauer and J. Mills, 1989
10 M. Gill, 1979

11   G. Bauer and J. Kobos, 1984
12   H. Davanloo, 1980
13   H. Strupp, 1977
14   P. Wachtel, 1986
15   O. Rank and S. Ferenczi, 1925
16   W. Reich, 1933
17   H. S. Sullivan, 1953
18   H. Racker, 1968
19   O. Kernberg et al., 1989
20   P. Wachtel, 1977
21   R. Schafer, 1983
22   M. Gill, 1982
23   B. Bird, 1972, p. 272

Chapter 2   The Importance of the Analysis of Transference in the Here and Now

1   L. Luborsky et al., 1971
2   D. Orlinsky and K. Howard, 1978
3   H. Davanloo, 1978
4   S. Budman and A. Gurman, 1988
5   H. Strupp, 1977
6   I. Yalom, 1986
7   R. Schafer, 1983
8   H. Strupp and J. Binder, 1984
9   K. Menninger, 1958, p. 63
10   E. Wolf, 1966
11   S. Freud, 1914
12   J. Strachey, 1934, p. 132
13   H. Strupp and J. Binder, 1984, p. 159
14   D. Kiesler, 1982
15   L. Stone, 1967, p. 35
16   P. Greenacre, 1959

17   H. S. Sullivan, 1954
18   M. Gill, 1982, p. 163
19   P. Wachtel, 1977
20   S. Freud, 1912a, p. 108

Chapter 3   Overview of Resistance

1   S. Freud, 1912a, p. 103
2   P. Dewald, 1964
3   R. Schafer, 1983
4   S. Freud, 1912a
5   H. S. Sullivan, 1947
6   E. Singer, 1965
7   H. Guntrip, 1969
8   D. Freebury, 1989
9   P. Wachtel, 1982a
10   H. Strupp and J. Binder, 1984
11   S. Freud, 1914, p. 155
12   S. Tarachow, 1963
13   R. Schafer, 1983, p. 75
14   R. Schafer, 1983, p. 168
15   S. Bach, 1985, p. 225

Chapter 4   Patient Resistance to the Analysis of Transference in the Here and Now

1   M. Gill, 1979
2   H. Strupp and J. Binder, 1984
3   R. Schafer, 1983
4   P. Wachtel, 1986
5   M. Gill and I. Hoffman, 1982
6   S. Freud, 1912a
7   E. Zetzel and W. Meissner, 1973

8   H. Racker, 1968
9   J. Sandler, 1976
10 S. Tarachow, 1963
11 A. Druck, 1989
12 I. Yalom, 1986
13 S. Levy, 1984
14 M. Gill, 1983
15 M. Gill, 1982
16 S. Freud, 1900
17 S. Freud, 1925
18 S. Ferenczi, 1925, p. 225
19 P. Heimann, 1956, p. 309
20 H. Strupp and J. Binder, 1984, p. 20
21 S. Lipton, 1977a
22 R. Waelder, 1930
23 I. Yalom, 1980
24 E. Singer, 1965
25 S. Freud, 1914, p. 151
26 S. Freud, 1912a, p. 101

Chapter 5   Therapist Resistance to Analysis of Transference in the Here and Now

1   S. Freud, 1912a
2   O. Rank and S. Ferenczi, 1925
3   J. Strachey, 1934, p. 364
4   W. R. Bion, 1967, p. 272
5   P. Wachtel, 1977
6   M. Gill, 1979
7   M. Gill, 1980-81
8   S. Lipton, 1977b
9   E. Glover, 1955
10 P. Gray, 1973, p. 480

11 J. Strachey, 1934, p. 158
12 R. Schafer, 1983
13 H. Strupp and J. Binder, 1984
14 P. Meadow, 1987
15 B. Bird, 1972
16 E. Glover, 1955, p. 108
17 O. Kernberg, 1975
18 E. Beier, 1966
19 S. Roth, 1987
20 K. Menninger, 1958
21 L. Epstein, 1979
22 O. Kernberg, et al., 1989
23 L. Tower, 1956
24 H. Racker, 1957
25 A. Issacharoff, 1979

Chapter 6   Overempahsis of Genetic Interpretation

1   J. Frank, 1974
2   R. Schafer, 1983
3   J. Reppen, 1982
4   H. Bruch, 1977
5   H. S. Sullivan, 1954
6   I. Yalom, 1975
7   F. Pine, 1985, p. 153
8   I. Yalom, 1980
9   C. Rycroft, 1966
10 O. Kernberg, et al., 1989
11 P. Dewald, 1964
12 F. Alexander and T. French, 1946
13 H. Strupp, 1973
14 S. Freud, 1914
15 P. Wachtel, 1982a, p. 46

Chapter 7   Constricted Therapist Activity

1   H. S. Sullivan, 1954, p. 54
2   H. S. Sullivan, 1954, p. 22
3   S. Lipton, 1977b
4   P. Wachtel, 1977
5   C. Goldin, 1985
6   H. Racker, 1968
7   F. Alexander, 1946
8   K. Eissler, 1953
9   J. Arlow, 1961
10 O. Fenichel, 1941, p. 86
11 H. S. Sullivan, 1954
12 A. M. Cooper, 1987
13 M. Gill, 1982
14 A. Druck, 1989
15 K. Menninger, 1958
16 A. Grey, 1988
17 G. Blanck and R. Blanck, 1974, p. 50
18 D. W. Winnicott, 1963
19 R. Carson, 1982
20 H. Strupp and J. Binder, 1984
21 P. Wachtel, 1986, p. 62
22 O. Kernberg, et al., 1989
23 W. Goldstein, 1991
24 D. Kiesler, 1982
25 J. Reppen, 1982
26 T. Dorpat, 1977
27 J. Strachey, 1934, p. 138
28 A. Issacharoff, 1979
29 P. Wachtel, 1982a
30 P. Wachtel, 1986, p. 64
31 H. Loewald, 1960

32   R. Schafer, 1983
33   O. Kernberg, 1982
34   R. Schafer, 1983, p. 5
35   G. Bauer and J. Kobos, 1990

Chapter 8   Overemphasis of Positive Transference

1   S. Freud, 1912a, p. 100
2   M. Gill and H. Muslin, 1976
3   J. McLaughlin, 1981
4   S. Freud, 1937, p. 388
5   L. Stone, 1967, p. 35
6   S. Roth, 1987
7   H. Loewald, 1960
8   R. Chessick, 1980
9   A. Druck, 1989
10   G. Blanck and R. Blanck, 1979
11   P. Heimann, 1956
12   H. Kohut, 1977
13   R. Schafer, 1983
14   D. W. Winnicott, 1963
15   B. Bird, 1972, p. 286

Chapter 9   Difficulties in Differentiating Transference from Nontransference

1   D. Wile, 1984
2   T. Szasz, 1963
3   T. Szasz, 1963, p. 438
4   I. Hoffman, 1983
5   M. Gill, 1983
6   H. Loewald, 1960, p. 32
7   J. McLaughlin, 1981
8   M. Gill, 1982, p. 85–86

9   P. Wachtel, 1980
10 I. Hoffman, 1985
11 M. Gill, 1982
12 P. Wachtel, 1986
13 M. Gill, 1980-81
14 O. Fenichel, 1941, pp. 72–73
15 M. Gill, 1979
16 M. Gill, 1979, pp. 281–282
17 P. Wachtel, 1980
18 R. Schafer, 1983

Chapter 10   Posture of Certainty

1   S. Freud, 1912b
2   R. Schafer, 1983
3   A. Cooper, 1987
4   I. Yalom, 1975
5   H. Kohut, 1971
6   H. Strupp and J. Binder, 1984, p. 48
7   P. Greenacre, 1959
8   H. Strupp and J. Binder, 1984
9   I. Hoffman, 1983
10 M. Gill, 1982
11 J. Reppen, 1982

Chapter 11   Premature Interpretation of Projection

1   L. Epstein, 1979
2   L. Epstein, 1979, p. 261
3   L. Epstein, 1979, p. 262
4   L. Sederer and J. Thorbeck, 1986
5   P. Meadow, 1987
6   L. Epstein, 1979, p. 265

Chapter 12   Interpretation

1   F. Pine, 1985
2   M. Basch, 1980
3   H. Kohut, 1984, p. 72
4   H. Strupp and J. Binder, 1984
5   J. Sandler, et al., 1971
6   J. Strachey, 1934
7   I. Yalom, 1975
8   H. S. Sullivan, 1954
9   P. Wachtel, 1977
10   M. Basch, 1980
11   S. Bach, 1985
12   L. Sederer and J. Thorbeck, 1986
13   L. Epstein, 1979
14   G. Blanck and R. Blanck, 1974, p. 326
15   G. Blanck and R. Blanck, 1974
16   S. Freud, 1913
17   T. French, 1946
18   S. Freud, 1940
19   L. Sederer and J. Thorbeck, 1986, pp. 696–697

Chapter 13   Working Through

1   S. Freud, 1914, p. 155
2   O. Fenichel, 1945, p. 31
3   A. Cooper, 1989
4   A. Cooper, 1989, p. 34
5   J. Marmor, 1979, pp. 351–352
6   S. Freud, 1914
7   P. Wachtel, 1982a
8   P. Wachtel, 1977
9   I. Yalom, 1975

Chapter 14   Resolution

1   H. Loewald, 1960
2   E. Singer, 1965
3   E. Singer, 1965, p. 277
4   M. Gill, 1982
5   E. Beier, 1966
6   D. Freebury, 1989, p. 774
7   M. Gill, 1983
8   I. Hoffman, 1983
9   I. Yalom, 1980
10   I. Yalom, 1980, p. 231
11   R. Schafer, 1983, p. 107

Chapter 15   Considerations on Implementing a Here-and-Now Approach

1   S. Freud, 1912b
2   L. Stone, 1961
3   S. Freud, 1913
4   S. Freud, 1916–1917
5   O. Kernberg, 1975
6   S. Tarachow, 1963
7   H. S. Sullivan, 1954, p. 164

References

Alexander, F. (1925). Review of *The Development of Psychoanalysis*, by O. Rank and S. Ferenczi. *International Journal of Psycho-Analysis* 6:484–496.

———— (1946). The principle of flexibility. In *Psychoanalytic Therapy: Principles and Application*, ed. F. Alexander and T. French, pp. 25–65. New York: Ronald.

Alexander, F., and French, T. (1946). *Psychoanalytic Therapy: Principles and Applications*. New York: Ronald.

Arlow, J. (1961). Silence and the theory of technique. *Journal of the American Psychoanalytic Association* 9:44–55.

Bach, S. (1985). *Narcissistic States and the Therapeutic Process*. Northvale, NJ: Jason Aronson.

Balint, M. (1968). *The Basic Fault: Therapeutic Aspects of Regression*. New York: Brunner/Mazel.

Basch, M. (1980). *Doing Psychotherapy*. New York: Basic Books.

Bauer, G., and Kobos, J. (1984). Short-term psychodynamic psychotherapy: reflections on the past and current practice. *Psychotherapy* 21:153–170.

_____ (1987). *Brief Therapy: Short-Term Psychodynamic Intervention.* Northvale, NJ: Jason Aronson.

_____ (1990). Common dilemmas in learning short-term psychodynamic psychotherapy. *Journal of College Student Psychotherapy* 5:57–73.

Bauer, G., and Mills, J. (1989). Use of transference in the here and now: patient and therapist resistance. *Psychotherapy* 26:112–119.

Beier, E. (1966). *The Silent Language of Psychotherapy.* Chicago: Aldine.

Bion, W. (1967). Notes on memory and desire. *The Psychoanalytic Forum* 2:271–281.

Bird, B. (1972). Notes on transference universal phenomenon and hardest part of the analysis. *Journal of the American Psychoanalytic Association* 20:267–300.

Blanck, G., and Blanck, R. (1974). *Ego Psychology: Theory and Practice.* New York: Columbia University Press.

_____ (1979). *Ego Psychology II.* New York: Columbia University Press.

Blanck, R., and Blanck, G. (1977). The transference object and the real object. *International Journal of Psycho-Analysis* 58:33–44.

Bromberg, P. (1984). The third ear. In *Clinical Perspectives on the Supervision of Psychoanalysis and Psychotherapy,* ed. L. Caligor, P. Bromberg, and J. Meltzer, pp. 29–44. New York: Plenum.

Bruch, H. (1977). Sullivan's concept of participant-observation (a symposium). *Contemporary Psychoanalysis* 13:347–386.

Budman, S., and Gurman, A. (1988). *Theory and Practice of Brief Therapy.* New York: Guilford.

Carson, R. (1982). Self-fulfilling prophecy, maladaptive behavior and psychotherapy. In *Handbook of Interpersonal Psychotherapy,* ed. J. Anchin and D. Kiesler, pp. 64–72. New York: Pergamon.

Chessick, R. (1980). *Freud Teaches Psychotherapy.* Indianapolis: Hackett.

Cooper, A. (1989). Working through. *Contemporary Psychoanalysis* 25:34–62.

Cooper, A. M. (1987). Changes in psychoanalytic ideas: transference interpretation. *Journal of the American Psychoanalytic Association* 35:77–98.

Davanloo, H. (1978). *Basic Principles and Techniques in Short-Term Dynamic Psychotherapy.* New York: Spectrum.

_____ (1980). *Short-Term Dynamic Psychotherapy.* New York: Jason Aronson.

Dewald, P. (1964). *Psychotherapy: A Dynamic Approach*. New York: Basic Books.

Dorpat, T. (1977). On neutrality. *International Journal of Psychoanalytic Psychotherapy* 6:39–64.

Druck, A. (1989). *Four Therapeutic Approaches to the Borderline Patient*. Northvale, NJ: Jason Aronson.

Eissler, K. (1953). The effect of the structure of the ego on psychoanalytic technique. *Journal of the American Psychoanalytic Association*. 1:104–143.

Epstein, L. (1979). The therapeutic use of countertransference data with borderline patients. *Contemporary Psychoanalysis* 15: 248–275.

Epstein, L., and Feiner, A. (1979). Countertransference: the therapist's contribution to treatment. *Contemporary Psychoanalysis* 15:489–513.

Fenichel, O. (1941). *Problems of Psychoanalytic Technique*. New York: Psychoanalytic Quarterly.

———— (1945). *The Psychoanalytic Theory of Neurosis*. New York: W.W. Norton.

Ferenczi, S. (1921). The further development of an active therapy in psychoanalysis. In *Further Contributions to the Theory and Technique of Psychoanalysis*, ed. J. Rickman, pp. 198–217. London: Hogarth, 1950.

———— (1925). Contra-indications to the "active" psychoanalytic technique. In *Further Contributions to the Theory and Technique of Psychoanalysis*, ed. J. Rickman, pp. 217–230. London: Hogarth, 1950.

———— (1928). The elasticity of psychoanalytic technique. In *Final Contributions to the Problems and Methods of Psychoanalysis*, ed. M. Balint, pp. 87–101. London: Hogarth, 1955.

Frank, J. (1974) *Persuasion and Healing*. 2nd ed. New York: Schocken.

Freebury, D. (1989). The therapeutic alliance: a psychoanalytic perspective. *Canadian Journal of Psychiatry* 34:772–774.

French, T. (1946). The dynamics of the therapeutic process. In *Psychoanalytic Therapy Principles and Application*, ed. F. Alexander and T. French, pp. 132–144. New York: Ronald.

Freud, S. (1900). The interpretation of dreams. *Standard Edition* 5.

———— (1905). Fragment of an analysis of a case of hysteria. *Standard Edition* 7:7–122.

_____ (1909). Notes upon a case of obsessional neurosis. *Standard Edition* 10:153–318.

_____ (1910). Observations on wild psychoanalysis. *Standard Edition* 11:219–227.

_____ (1912a). The dynamics of transference. *Standard Edition* 12:99–108.

_____ (1912b). Recommendations to physicians practicing psychoanalysis. *Standard Edition* 12:111–120.

_____ (1913). On beginning the treatment. *Standard Edition* 12:123–144.

_____ (1914). Remembering, repeating and working through. *Standard Edition* 12:145–157.

_____ (1915). Observations on transference love. *Standard Edition* 12:157–172.

_____ (1916–1917). Introductory lectures in psychoanalysis. *Standard Edition* 15,16.

_____ (1925). An autobiographical study. *Standard Edition* 20:7–74.

_____ (1926). The question of lay analysis. *Standard Edition* 20:183–258.

_____ (1937). Analysis terminable and interminable. *International Journal of Psycho-Analysis* 18:373–405.

_____ (1940). An outline of psychoanalysis. *Standard Edition* 23:139–207.

Friedman, L. (1978). Trends in the psychoanalytic theory of treatment. *Psychoanalytic Quarterly* 47:524–567.

Gill, M. (1979). The analysis of the transference. *Journal of the American Psychoanalytic Association* 27:263–288.

_____ (1980–1981). The analysis of transference: a critique of Fenichel's *Problems of Psychoanalytic Technique*. *International Journal of Psychoanalytic Psychotherapy* 8:45–56.

_____ (1982). *The Analysis of Transference*. Vol. 1. New York: International Universities Press.

_____ (1983). The interpersonal paradigm and the degree of the therapist's involvement. *Contemporary Psychoanalysis* 19:200–237.

Gill, M., and Hoffman, I. (1982). *Analysis of Transference*. Vol. 2. New York: International Universities Press.

Gill, M., and Muslin, H. (1976). Early interpretation of transference. *Journal of the American Psychoanalytic Association* 24:779–794.

Glover, E. (1955). *The Technique of Psychoanalysis*. New York: International Universities Press.

Goldberg, A. (1985). The definition and role of interpretation. In *Progress in Self Psychology*. Vol. 1, ed. A. Goldberg, pp. 62–68. New York: Guilford.

Goldin, V. (1985). Problems of technique. In *Treating the Oedipal Patient in Brief Psychotherapy*, ed. A. Horner, pp. 55–74. Northvale, NJ: Jason Aronson.

Goldstein, W. (1991). Clarification of projective identification. *American Journal of Psychiatry* 148:153–161.

Gray, P. (1973). Psychoanalytic technique and the ego's capacity for viewing intrapsychic activity. *Journal of the American Psychoanalytic Association* 21:474–495.

Greenacre, P. (1954). The role of transference. *Journal of the American Psychoanalytic Association* 2:671–684.

———— (1959). Certain technical problems in the transference relationship. *Journal of the American Psychoanalytic Association* 7:484–502.

Greenson, R. (1965). The working alliance and the transference neurosis. *Psychoanalytic Quarterly* 34:155–181.

———— (1967). *The Technique and Practice of Psychoanalysis*. New York: International Universities Press.

Grey, A. (1988). Sullivan's contribution to psychoanalysis. *Contemporary Psychoanalysis* 24:548–576.

Guntrip, H. (1969). *Schizoid Phenomena, Object-Relations and the Self*. New York: International Universities Press.

Gustafson, J. (1986). *The Complex Secret of Brief Psychotherapy*. New York: Norton.

Heimann, P. (1956). Dynamics of transference interpretations. *International Journal of Psycho-Analysis* 37:303–310.

Hoffman, I. (1983). The patient as interpreter of the analyst's experience. *Contemporary Psychoanalysis* 19:389–422.

———— (1985). Merton M. Gill. In *Beyond Freud: A Study of Modern Psychoanalytic Theorists*, ed. J. Reppen, pp. 135–174. Hillsdale, NJ: Analytic Press.

Hunt, W., and Issacharoff, A. (1977). Heinrich Racker and countertransference theory. *Journal of the American Academy of Psychoanalysis* 5:95–105.

Issacharoff, A. (1979). Barriers to knowing. In *Countertransference*, ed. L. Epstein and A. Feiner, pp. 27–43. New York: Jason Aronson.

Jung, C. G. (1933). *Modern Man in Search of a Soul.* New York: Harvest Books.

Kasin, E. (1977). Sullivan's concept of participant-observation (a symposium). *Contemporary Psychoanalysis* 13:347–386.

Kermode, F. (1985). Freud and interpretation. *International Review of Psycho-Analysis* 12:3–12.

Kernberg, O. (1975). *Borderline Conditions and Pathological Narcissism.* New York: Jason Aronson.

———— (1976). *Object-Relations Theory and Clinical Psychoanalysis.* New York: Jason Aronson.

———— (1982). The theory of psychoanalytic psychotherapy. In *Curative Factors in Dynamic Psychotherapy*, ed. S. Slipp, pp. 21–43. New York: McGraw-Hill.

Kernberg, O., Selzer, M., Koenigsberg, H., et al. (1989). *Psychodynamic Psychotherapy of Borderline Patients.* New York: Basic Books.

Kiesler, D. (1982). Confronting the client–therapist relationship in psychotherapy. In *Interpersonal Psychotherapy*, ed. J. Anchin and D. Kiesler, pp. 274–295. New York: Pergamon.

Kohut, H. (1971). *The Analysis of the Self.* New York: International Universities Press.

———— (1977). *The Restoration of the Self.* New York: International Universities Press.

———— (1984). *How Does Analysis Cure?* Chicago: University of Chicago Press.

Levy, S. (1984). *Principles of Interpretion.* New York: Jason Aronson.

Lipton, S. (1977a). Clinical observations on resistance to transference. *International Journal of Psycho-Analysis* 58:468–472.

———— (1977b). The advantages of Freud's technique shown in his analysis of the rat man. *International Journal of Psycho-Analysis* 58:255–273.

Loewald, H. (1960). On the therapeutic action of psychoanalysis. *International Journal of Psycho-Analysis* 41:16–33.

Luborsky, L., Chandler, M., Auerbach, A. H., et al. (1971). Factors influencing the outcome of psychotherapy: a review of quanititative research. *Psychological Bulletin* 75:145–185.

Malan, D. (1963). *A Study of Brief Psychotherapy.* New York: Plenum.

_____ (1976). *Frontier of Brief Psychotherapy*. New York: Plenum.

Malcolm, J. (1981). *Psychoanalysis: The Impossible Mission*. New York: Alfred Knopf.

Marmor, J. (1979). Change in psychoanalytic treatment. *Journal of the American Academy of Psychoanalysis* 7:345–357.

McLaughlin, J. (1981). Transference, psychic reality, and countertransference. *Psychoanalytic Quarterly* 4:639–664.

Meadow, P. (1987). The myth of the impersonal analyst. *Modern Psychoanalysis* 12:131–150.

Menninger, K. (1958). *Theory of Psychoanalytic Technique*. New York: Basic Books.

Orlinsky, D. E., and Howard, K. I. (1978). The relation of process to outcome in psychotherapy. In *Handbook of Psychotherapy and Behavior Change: An Empirical Analysis*, 2nd ed., ed. S. L. Garfield and A. E. Bergin, pp. 283–329. New York: Wiley.

Ornstein, P., and Ornstein A. (1985). Clinical understanding and explaining: the empathic vantage point. In *Progress in Self Psychology*, vol. 1, ed. A. Goldberg, pp. 43–61. New York: Guilford.

Pine, F. (1985). *Developmental Theory and Clinical Process*. New Haven: Yale University Press.

Racker, H. (1957). The meanings and uses of countertransference. *Psychoanalytic Quarterly* 26:303–357.

_____ (1968). *Transference and Countertransference*. New York: International Universities Press.

Rank, O., and Ferenczi, S. (1925). *The Development of Psychoanalysis*. Trans. C. Newton. New York: Nervous and Mental Diseases.

Reich, W. (1933). *Character Analysis*. Trans. T. Wocfus. Rangeley, ME: Orgonics Institute Press.

Reppen, J. (1982). Merton Gill: an interview. *The Psychoanalytic Review* 69:167–190.

Roth, S. (1987). *Psychotherapy: The Art of Wooing Nature*. Northvale, NJ: Jason Aronson.

Rycroft, C. (1966). *Psychoanalysis Observed*. London: Constable.

Sandler, J. (1976). Countertransference and role-responsiveness. *International Review of Psycho-Analysis* 3:43–47.

Sandler, J., Dare, C., and Holder, A. (1971). Basic psychoanalytic concepts. Vol. 10: interpretations and other interventions. *British Journal of Psychiatry* 118:53–59.

Sandler, J., Holder, A., Kawenoka, M., et al. (1969). Notes on some theoretical and clinical aspects of transference. *International Journal of Psycho-Analysis* 50:633–645.

Schafer, R. (1983). *The Analytic Attitude*. New York: Basic Books.

Sederer, L., and Thorbeck, J. (1986). First do no harm: short-term inpatient psychotherapy of the borderline patient. *Hospital and Community Psychiatry* 37:692–697.

Semrad, E. (1980). On therapy and in therapy. In *Semrad, The Heart of a Therapist*, ed. S. Rako and H. Mazer, pp. 99–127. Northvale, NJ: Jason Aronson.

Sifneos, P. (1987). *Short-term Dynamic Psychotherapy*, 2nd ed. New York: Plenum.

Singer, E. (1965). *Key Concepts in Psychotherapy*. New York: Basic Books.

Stone, L. (1961). *The Psychoanalytic Situation*. New York: International Universities Press.

———— (1967). The psychoanalytic situation and transference. *Journal of the American Psychoanalytic Association* 15:3–58.

———— (1973). On resistance to the psychoanalytic process. *Psychoanalysis and Contemporary Science* 2:42–73.

Strachey, J. (1934). The nature of the therapeutic action of psychoanalysis. *International Journal of Psycho-Analysis* 15: 127–159.

Strupp, H. (1973). *Psychotherapy: Clinical, Research, and Theoretical Issues*. New York: Jason Aronson.

———— (1977). A reformation of the dynamics of the therapist's contribution. In *Effective Psychotherapy: A Handbook of Research*, ed. A. Gurman and A. Razin, pp. 3–22. New York: Pergamon.

Strupp, H., and Binder, J. (1984). *Psychotherapy in a New Key*. New York: Basic Books.

Sullivan, H. S. (1947). *Conceptions of Modern Psychiatry*. New York: W. W. Norton.

———— (1953). *The Interpersonal Theory of Psychiatry*. New York: W. W. Norton.

———— (1954). *The Psychiatric Interview*. New York: W. W. Norton.

Szasz, T. (1963). The concept of transference. *International Journal of Psycho-Analysis* 44:432–443.

Tarachow, S. (1963). *An Introduction to Psychotherapy*. New York: International Universities Press.

Tower, L. (1956). Countertransference. *Journal of the American Psychoanalytic Association* 4:224–255.

Wachtel, P. (1977). *Psychoanalysis and Behavior Therapy*. New York: Basic Books.

_____ (1980). Transference, schema, and assimilation: the relevance of Piaget to the psychoanalytic theory of transference. *The Annals of Psychoanalysis* 8:59–76.

_____ (1982a). Interpersonal learning and active intervention. In *Handbook of Interpersonal Psychotherapy*, ed. J. Anchin and D. Kiesler, pp. 46–63. New York: Pergamon.

_____ (1982b). Vicious cycles. *Contemporary Psychoanalysis* 18:259–272.

_____ (1986). On the limits of therapeutic neutrality. *Contemporary Psychoanalysis* 22:60–70.

Waelder, R. (1930). The principle of multiple function. *Psychoanalytic Quarterly* 5:45–62.

White, M.J. (1952). Sullivan and treatment. In *The Contributions of Harry Stack Sullivan*, ed. P. Mullahy, pp. 117–150. New York: Hermitage House.

Wile, D. (1984). Kohut, Kernberg, and accusatory interpretations. *Psychotherapy* 21:353–364.

Winnicott, D. W. (1949). Hate in the countertransference. *International Journal of Psycho-Analysis* 30:69–74.

_____ (1963). From dependence towards independence in the development of the individual. In *The Maturational Processes and the Facilitating Environment*, pp. 83–92. New York: International Universities Press.

Wolf, E. (1966). Learning theory and psychoanalysis. *British Journal of Medical Psychology* 39:1–10.

Yalom, I. (1975). *The Theory and Practice of Group Psychotherapy*. New York: Basic Books.

_____ (1980). *Exisential Psychotherapy*. New York: Basic Books.

_____ (1986). Interpersonal learning. In *American Psychiatric Association Annual Review*, ed. A. Frances and R. Hales, 5:699–713. Washington, DC: American Psychiatric Press.

Young, D., and Beier, E. (1982). Being asocial in social places: giving the client a new experience. In *Handbook of Interpersonal Psychotherapy*, ed. J. Anchin and D. Kiesler, pp. 262–273. New York: Pergamon.

Zetzel, E. (1956). The concept of transference. In *The Capacity for Emotional Growth*, pp. 168–181. New York: International Universities Press, 1970.

Zetzel, E., and Meissner, W. (1973). *Basic Concepts of Psychoanalytic Psychiatry*. New York: Basic Books.

Index